GOLF

It's All Mental

by

Larry Eichenauer

Published by
Heritage Publishing.US
Bradenton, Florida
www.heritagepublishingus.com

Contents

Foreword

I have often contemplated how I can casually tap in a 3-foot putt with one hand and yet, if I take my time, and follow a routine, I often miss a short putt. What is it about our mental processing that made the tap-in easy and the normal routine difficult? How can a person look at the golf ball for a fraction of a second and hit it squarely nearly every time. But, when you take your time, using a structured setup, the ball is often struck off line. It's time to seek a better understanding of how the mind works.

The normal response by most psychologists and golfers would attribute this lack of consistency to tension. That may be true, but could the reason be that the brain functions more accurately, when the action is performed spontaneously. Similarly, a hockey player can turn around 180 degrees and slap a puck in an exact intended direction. Little thought was involved. It was an impulsive action. Consider a baseball player swinging at a ball moving 100 mph. There is no time to formulate any thought. It is entirely reactionary. How can we perform these impulsive movements and produce such accurate results?

In this book, I will provide insight for how the brain is capable of such extraordinary feats. We are overlooking the potential of the thinking process that allows us to do what often seems impossible. Over the past 50 years, golf has become so structured. Do we have a natural ability to perform a beautiful golf swing that requires less thinking? Is it possible for the golf swing to be more impulsive? Every activity we perform that is done in a casual manner normally produces accurate results. If the golf swing could become more reactionary, I believe we could all improve.

In the first chapter, I will provide information for how the brain functions in our normal lives and in the golf swing. By understanding the brain, it provides us with greater insight for how we can train our brains to function at a higher level. The best players in golf have used many of the techniques I will be discussing for gaining accuracy and consistency. Golf is the only sport where the target is something other than what you are focusing on. This dilemma can only be overcome by using visualization and intense focus. Both of these topics are discussed in detail and I will offer new concepts for how the brain can be taught to improve the way we use visualization and focus. I will offer solutions to seeing the target rather than the ball at the moment of impact.

Golf can be a mental challenge. Confidence is the key to being successful at golf. There are ways to improve and maintain confidence. We must train our brains a certain way to achieve the confidence needed for golf. Included is an entire chapter providing solutions for playing with more confidence.

Every player could improve if they used their time for practicing in a more creative way. Everyone complains that they practice better than they play. There are reasons why this is true. I will offer solutions to correct this Dr. Jekyll and Mr. Hyde analogy for the range vs. the course.

In today's world, golf is considered a mental sport. This may be true because psychologists have written more books about golf than all other sports combined. In addition, many professional golfers often seek advice from several renowned psychologists. They have become a second coach for many of the well-known PGA and LPGA players.

After learning a better procedure for practice, it is time to "take it to the course". All the practice in the world does not produce guaranteed results, although Ben Hogan may have had a different opinion since he practiced constantly searching for the perfect swing. You can develop a near perfect swing, but once you begin a round of golf, you soon realize that this game is more about how you control your mind than swinging a club.

One entire chapter is dedicated to training the mind and body using special drills. The golf swing is segmented into 6 parts with photos to illustrate how to perform these specific drills to orchestrate a better swing.

I conclude the book with "Final Thoughts" reviewing current golfers and a few historical figures, deciphering what factors produced some of the greatest players of all time. These players possess(ed) immense talent but in the end their greatness is attributed to how well they manage(d) the mental part of their game. Their mental skills are what all golfers need to understand if they desire to take their game to the next level.

Chapter 1

How We Think

"Competitive golf is played mainly on a five-and-a-half inch course... The space between the ears."

Bobby Jones

Having read many books about Ben Hogan, I have become intrigued with his personality and his pursuit for perfection. No professional golfer will ever challenge his tenacity to attain the ideal golf swing. In 1946, Ben Hogan announced he discovered a secret to having a great swing. He said he could not disclose any information about his secret since he didn't want his competitors to know. This cloud of secrecy went on for years. Finally, in 1955, Life Magazine offered Hogan $10,000 to tell his secret to the world. Hogan wanted more money, but agreed. After the article was published, many suggested he did not reveal his true secret for his excellent swing. Hogan later admitted he would need to be paid $100,000 for divulging his real secret in his golf swing. No magazine would succumb to his demand, and so the secret was most likely taken with him to his grave. Out of respect, his friends Ken Ventura and Tommy Bolt would not release what they knew about Ben Hogan's swing. Even though he may have mentored them, it is not certain he divulged the "real" secret. In the book, "Ben Hogan's Secret Fundamental" written by Larry Miller, who had close ties to these two great golfers, mentions the likely possibilities for his secret(s).

This leads me to the start of this chapter. One thing that Hogan did more than anyone was to outwork the competition. He said, to be successful as a golfer you must "dig it out of the dirt". Of course he was referring to hitting countless golf balls, until it became so automatic that eventually no thought was required to perform the motion of the ideal swing. Obviously, it was how he rehearsed the golf swing that was his "real" secret. He spent a lifetime training his mind to repeat the same motions every time he would swing the club. In reality, there can be no other conclusion to his secret. Accepting the fact that we can see the swing happening right in front of us by viewing videos of Hogan's swing, there can be no secret waiting to be told. We have had years to diagnose his swing. It's what we don't see that is the secret. Training the mind to swing a golf club is a secret in itself. It's in the mind of all of us to perform to the best of our ability. It's how we train our mind that distinguishes excellence. Granted, some people are born with special talents, and this mental training takes a short cut. If we all train enough we can be good at something, even though the odds may not be in our favor. Ben Hogan was born with raw talent and he knew how to produce the best results by the way he would, "dig it out of the dirt".

So if we conclude that this was likely his real secret, we need to consider this as the ideal way to achieve excellence. If we are going to train our minds properly, we must first understand how the mind works.

The brain is the third largest organ in our body. It is preceded by the skin and liver. The average brain weighs a little less than 3 pounds. It contains approximately 100 billion neurons and over 100 trillion synaptic connections. The cerebrum is the largest part of the brain consisting of four parts: frontal lobe, temporal lobe, parietal lobe, and occipital lobe. The lower back of the brain includes the cerebellum. **(See FIG.1).**

The brain has two hemispheres that work together. The left and right side of the brain are joined at the bottom portion by the corpus callosum. The two sides function and work together by the corpus callosum sending messages from one side to the other. The illustration shows the different functions provided by specific parts of the brain. **(See FIG. 2)** You can see where one section of the brain may be responsible for a certain function and it is also supported within another portion. The same is true for the different hemispheres. Many parts of the brain are intertwined in controlling our body functions and memory.

The brain is very complex and it is capable of doing far more than we can imagine. It has been suggested we use 10% of our brain's capacity. This statement is not true, since this was proposed 100 years ago when brain research was mainly done with mice. The brain of the mouse cannot be compared to the human brain. We actually use almost 100% of our brain, although we are not fully aware of its true potential. We still know little about what the brain is capable of. We need to find ways to tap into this unknown potential that could expand our abilities to think and perform.

Computers have the ability to absorb almost endless information, but they lack so many biological capabilities that the brain possesses. To name a few: The senses of taste, touch, smell, sight, and hearing. There are also emotions, imagination, creativity, and of course, reproduction. The brain functions using chemical and electrical connections, whereas the computer is solely electrical. The brain transfers information through neurons. The neurons are connected to other neurons by nerve pathways called dendrites and axons. Dendrites receive impulses and axons send impulses. The neurons are the nerve centers that route the information they receive. **(See FIGS. 3&4)** Before information can be transmitted to the axons, synapse connectors are stimulated by a chemical that connects the synapse connection. Basically, the synapse is similar to an on/off switch.

Most neurons are somewhat spherical in shape and their diameter is smaller than the human hair. Some neurons have over 10,000 connections (synapses). **(See FIG. 5)** Neurons, dendrites, and axons are interwoven throughout the brain. Some of this information transfer stays in the brain for things such as memory, intelligence, four of the five senses, certain emotions, personality, reasoning, and creativity. For the rest of our body functions, these neurons are ultimately connected to the brain stem, which is connected to the spinal cord. The spinal cord transmits information from the brain to every part of our body. The spinal cord has nerve bundles that branch out to specific muscles and organs. The nerve bundles receive messages from the brain and they can also send messages back to the brain. All this information is constantly being sent and received to every part of our body and the transfer of information is almost instantaneous. **(See FIG. 6)**

I just explained a quick summary and it starts to become clear why we know so little about the brain. The brain is extremely complex!

Golf is a mental sport. Most people would agree it likely requires more mental control and knowledge than any

THE HUMAN BRAIN

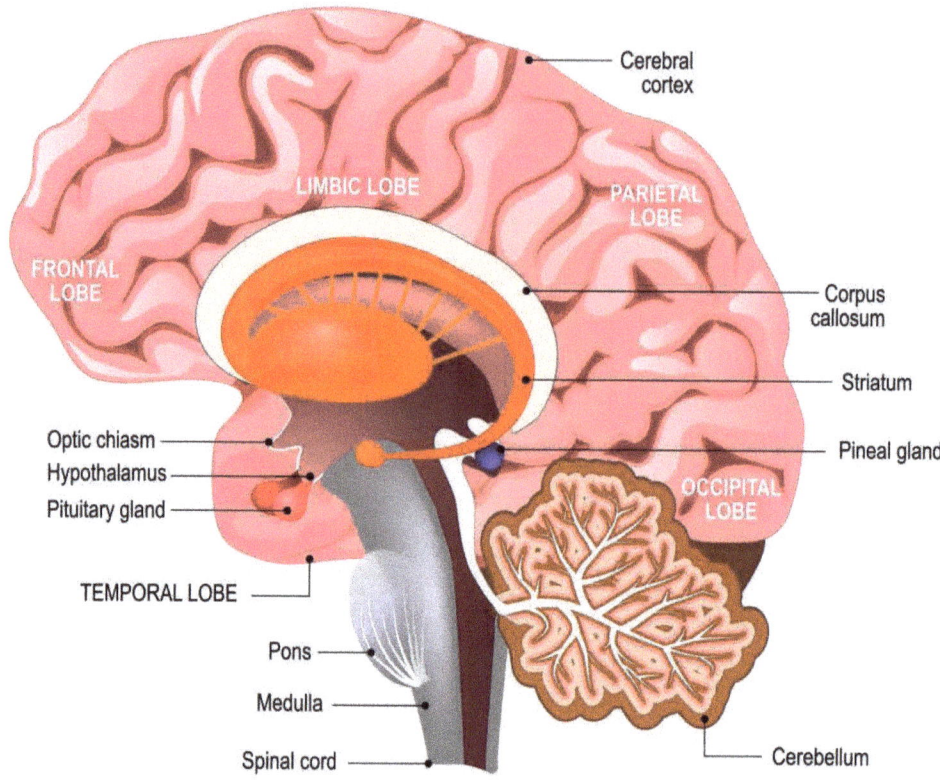

Cerebral cortex

LIMBIC LOBE

PARIETAL LOBE

FRONTAL LOBE

Corpus callosum

Striatum

Optic chiasm

Hypothalamus

Pituitary gland

Pineal gland

OCCIPITAL LOBE

TEMPORAL LOBE

Pons

Medulla

Spinal cord

Cerebellum

FIG. 1

The midbrain controls most of our basic functions, while the wrinkled portion (cerebrum) controls thinking, memory, and reasoning. The cerebrum is composed of both gray matter and white matter. Gray matter is composed of mainly neuron cells, and white matter is composed of mainly axons. Axons are carriers of information and they have a protective layer called myelin, which is white. The wrinkles in the cerebrum is likely the result of how the brain develops. The white and gray matter work together better with this wrinkled highway pattern.

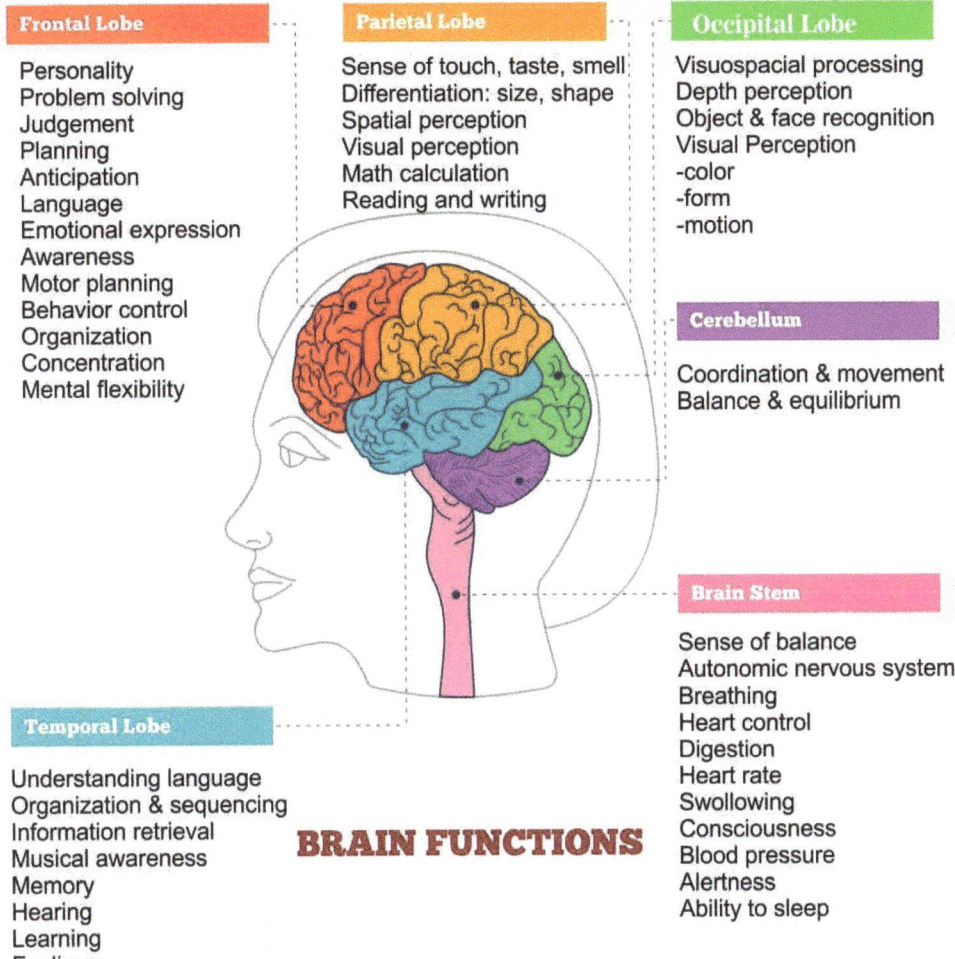

Frontal Lobe

Personality
Problem solving
Judgement
Planning
Anticipation
Language
Emotional expression
Awareness
Motor planning
Behavior control
Organization
Concentration
Mental flexibility

Parietal Lobe

Sense of touch, taste, smell
Differentiation: size, shape
Spatial perception
Visual perception
Math calculation
Reading and writing

Occipital Lobe

Visuospacial processing
Depth perception
Object & face recognition
Visual Perception
-color
-form
-motion

Cerebellum

Coordination & movement
Balance & equilibrium

Temporal Lobe

Understanding language
Organization & sequencing
Information retrieval
Musical awareness
Memory
Hearing
Learning
Feelings

Brain Stem

Sense of balance
Autonomic nervous system
Breathing
Heart control
Digestion
Heart rate
Swollowing
Consciousness
Blood pressure
Alertness
Ability to sleep

BRAIN FUNCTIONS

FIG. 2

All the functions shown are not isolated to just one part of the brain. Information is shared between parts of the brain to help formulate an action or thought. The neurons and synapses are intertwined throughout the brain for improving our thinking process. Humans use nearly 100% of the brain's capacity and yet neurologist admit we still have much to learn about what it is capable of and how it works.

NEURON COMPONENTS

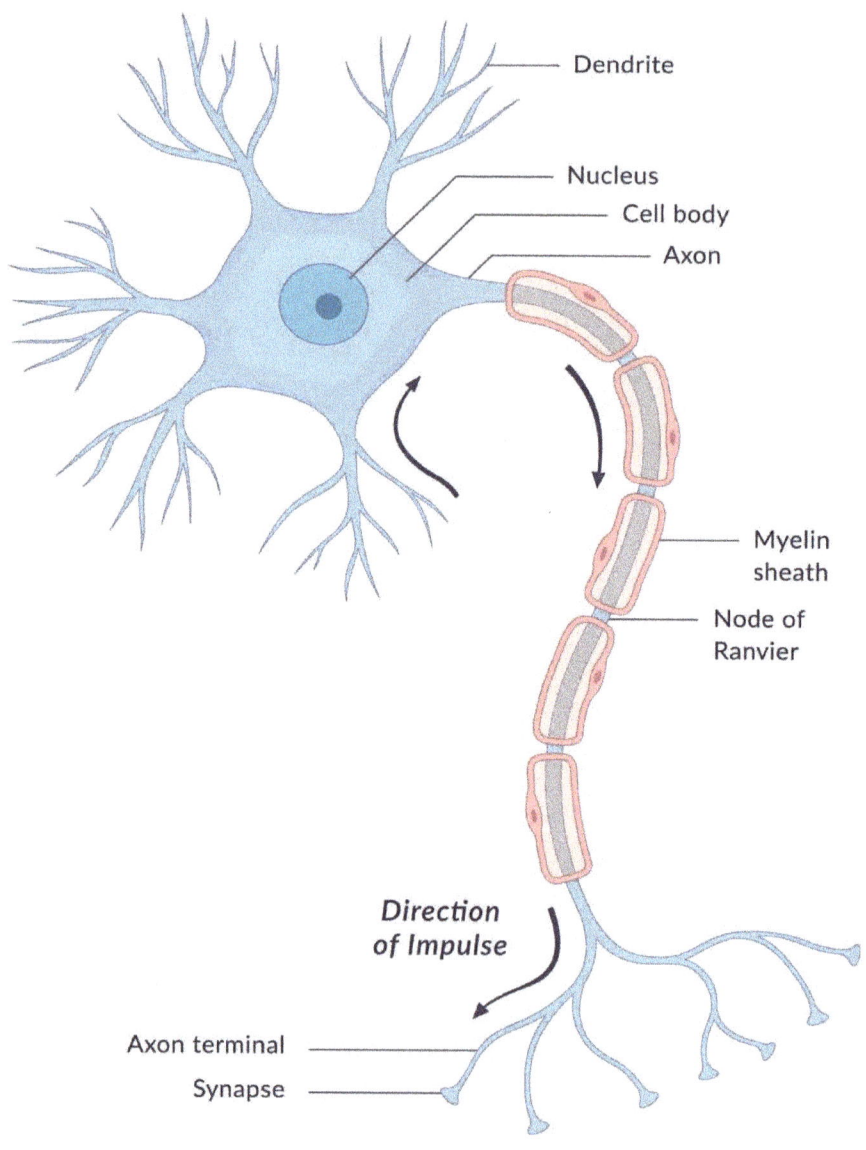

Dendrite

Nucleus

Cell body

Axon

Myelin sheath

Node of Ranvier

Direction of Impulse

Axon terminal

Synapse

FIG. 3

There are 100 billion neurons and 100 trillion synapses in our brain. The size of each neuron cell is approximately 10 microns (1/2500").

NEURON ILLUSTRATION

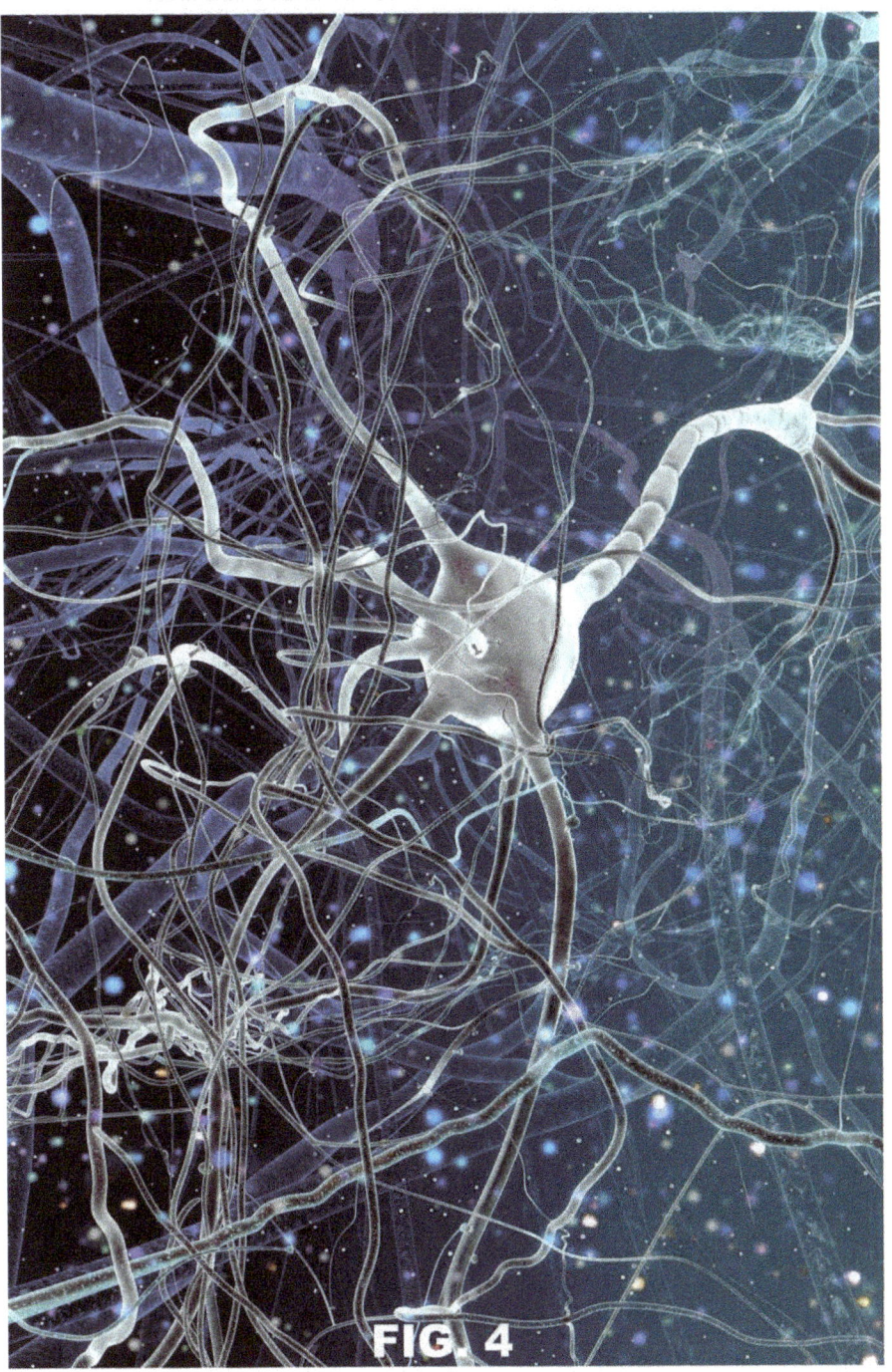

FIG. 4

SYNAPSE
and
NEUROTRANSMISSION

(the presynaptic neuron releases a neurotransmitter, which
activates receptors on the postsynaptic neuron)

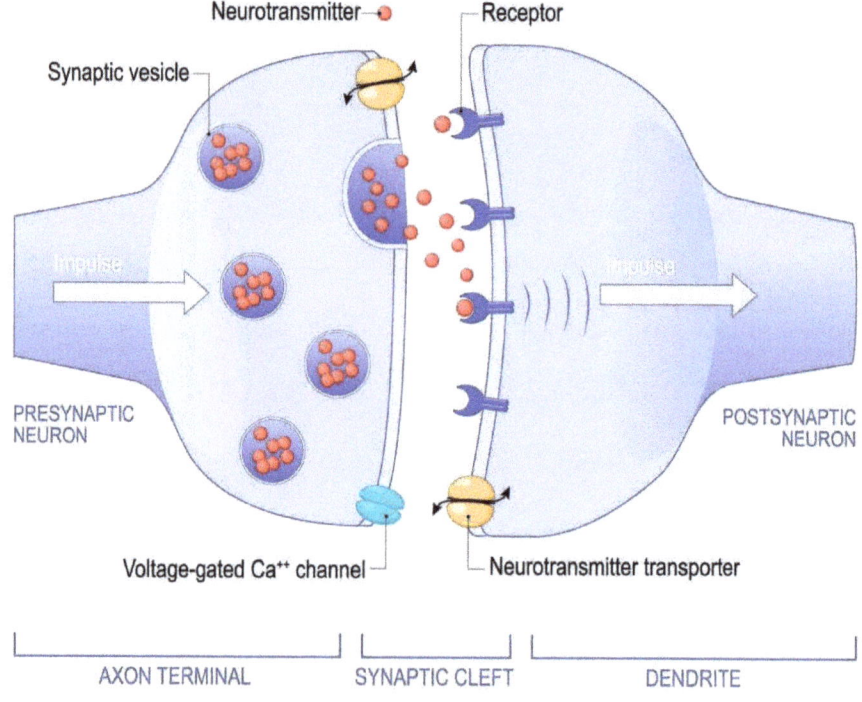

FIG. 5

Information is transferred between neurons by means of electrical
and chemical synapse connections. An electronic impulse "action
potential" triggers chemical transmitters (neurotransmitters) to
connect the opposing synapse to relay messages interspersed
throughout the brain.

CENTRAL NERVOUS SYSTEM

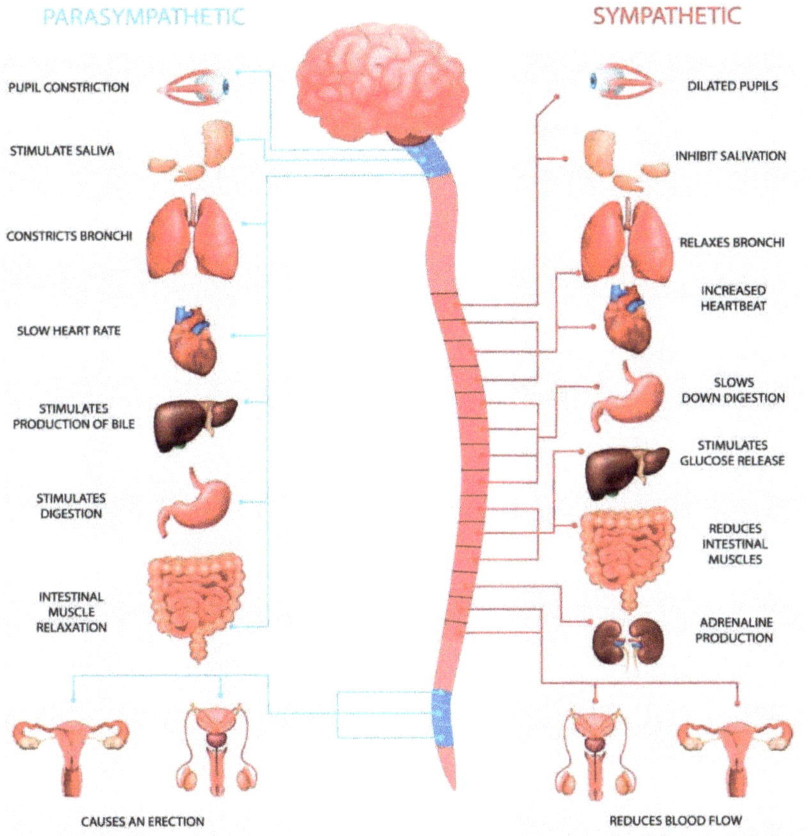

PARASYMPATHETIC   SYMPATHETIC

PUPIL CONSTRICTION   DILATED PUPILS

STIMULATE SALIVA   INHIBIT SALIVATION

CONSTRICTS BRONCHI   RELAXES BRONCHI

                                                          INCREASED
                                                          HEARTBEAT

SLOW HEART RATE

                                                          SLOWS
                                                          DOWN DIGESTION

STIMULATES   STIMULATES
PRODUCTION OF BILE   GLUCOSE RELEASE

STIMULATES   REDUCES
DIGESTION   INTESTINAL
                                                          MUSCLES

INTESTINAL
MUSCLE   ADRENALINE
RELAXATION   PRODUCTION

CAUSES AN ERECTION   REDUCES BLOOD FLOW

FIG. 6

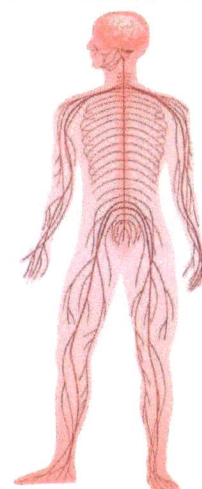

Motor neurons transmit electrical impulses from specific locations in the spinal cord to various muscles and organs throughout the body. Most basic functions of the body are originally sent from the lower parts of the brain and brain stem (pons and madulla oblongatta). Sympathetic nerves control more actice processes in the body and the parasympathetic nerves control the body in a restful state. Both nervous systems work together at all times.

other sport. To be successful at golf, the brain must be able to move muscles and maintain balance to near perfection. In golf, the brain must control mental and visual focus, must be creative, must be analytical, must control emotions, and must control disposition by being calm and resolute. So, if you want to improve your golf game, you must focus on the every one of these functions. The mind must be trained to produce better physical results. This is what Ben Hogan did in his effort to perfect the golf swing.

In reality, everything we do is mental. The mind controls all the actions and non-actions we deal with every day of our lives. It's all about making the right decisions involving our surroundings, which includes how we relate to other people. These decisions can affect both present and future events. Our mind is capable of predicting future events based on our memory of past experiences. Our ability to predict may not always be accurate but it is our anticipation that drives us to set goals that will determine success or failure. A better understanding of how the brain works will help us make better decisions, and help us perform certain activities, such as golf.

Golf can be very complicated. It is the most mentally challenging of all the sports. During a round of golf you are faced with countless decisions. How we approach these circumstances will determine how well we perform. Here are examples of some of these challenging decisions:
-What is the wind speed and direction?
-Do I hit a draw or a fade shot?
-How should I approach the green?

-How much break on the downhill putt?
-What club should I choose for a certain chip shot?
-Should I putt when just off the green?
-Do I choose the driver or play a safe shot?
-What club do I use for a certain yardage?
-Do I layup, or go for the green?
-What club do I choose to avoid the bunker?

This list could fill 50 pages of this book. Every shot in golf is different. If we are going to improve, we need to look into the minds of the greatest golfers of all time. They may hold the secrets we are searching for. For some reason, these players discovered something that others have yet to ascertain. Was it, their tenacity to practice more, their mental focus, their natural ability, better golf instruction, or their desire to win? I will analyze these special skills throughout the remaining chapters of this book.

Have you ever noticed when you work on a difficult tedious project it seems easier to accomplish if you listen to music? Our mind functions better when our subconscious is engaged in some form of rhythm. You might say this is due to the fact that the mind is lured into a sense of calm. When rhythm is introduced, the brain will not only process information better, but it also creates harmony in movement. If rhythm is added to your current lifestyle, you would likely avoid many difficulties.

Everything about golf lends itself to rhythm. Tempo and timing are essential ingredients for a good golf swing. If you can surround yourself with rhythm while playing golf, it will improve tempo and timing, and it will prevent negative thoughts from invading your mind. If you have a beat to your routine, it will help you establish a smoother swing. To obtain this beat, just add the melody of a favorite song to your setup routine and your swing. You can also enhance practice sessions by listening to music, especially when working on tempo and timing. Include a form of rhythm for chipping and putting as well.

Ben Hogan used to follow a strict routine in golf and in everything he did. He said having a routine in his normal lifestyle improved his game. At his home course he would sit at the same table and chair at the club restaurant every time. He was also very punctual and performed activities at the same time each day, such as practicing. By following a regimented lifestyle he felt like he had rhythm in his life, which he said influenced his state of mind for playing golf. There is something about a routine that adds harmony and reduces stress in our lives. Have you ever arrived at the golf course late and you had to rush to check in, pay for your round, rapidly put on your golf shoes, and jog to your cart? You had no time to practice and warm up. You barely had time to make your 8:00 tee-time. Your foursome group is telling you to hurry because you are next to tee-off. We have all had a similar occurrence and it will normally take 3 to 4 holes to get the heart rate down and regain mental focus. And, by being stressed, you will always score poorly. Taking deep breaths will not work. The mind is a creature of habit. Being punctual and following a routine, just like Ben

Hogan, is part of maintaining your mental well-being for golf.

The more rhythm you create, the more your mind will be clear for thought and functionality. If you want to be relaxed when you tee-off on the first hole, always follow a slower routine. Many professionals will slow everything down the day they play golf. Many great players follow a routine that starts when they wake up each game day by walking slower, talking slower, eating slower, driving slower, and then continue this slower rhythm when they arrive at the course and warm up. This sets the pace for the entire day, and it will encourage less stress to start the round. The mind and body will function at the highest levels only if you attain a feeling of calm and control for the challenges you may be facing.

The basal ganglia, motor cortex, and cerebellum all work together to make us tap our foot while listening to music. These parts of the brain allow us to feel rhythm when playing an instrument or listening to your favorite music. As I stated previously, our mind performs better when you feel rhythm. For example, you're working out at the gym and you feel like you don't want to continue your workout because you are getting tired. However, if you are watching a TV monitor or you are listening to music, the time seems to fly by, and as a result you can continue to work out twice as long as you would without these devices. What has changed to induce this supposed added strength and endurance? Your physical ability has not changed, so what changed? The brain has changed how it functions. By supplying the brain with a subconscious focus different from the workout, the brain was not telling your muscles that they were getting tired. The communication to the muscles was distracted by the thought of your mind focused on music or TV. Your memory in your mind recalls other times you did these forms of entertainment and it produced a feeling of relaxation and escape. The mind was in a different place so your muscles were not receiving the normal instructions of being tired. The communication going back to the brain was not being received. Remember, the nerves in the body receive and send message back to the brain. For example, your heart could not restore normal heart rate if communication between the nerves did not work both ways. This is just one example of how we can control our brain and there are many other ways as well. Your golf game can be reshaped by just finding new ways to manage the brain.

The analogy of working out with music and other media is no different than adding a good routine and visualization to your golf swing. There is little difference in how the brain will function with a routine or with music or other types of background reinforcement. The routine provides a subliminal and rhythmic method for improving mental ability. It is the best way to promote a smooth automatic swing. I will discuss the routine in a later chapter.

Right brain vs. left brain has become a hot topic for sports and general discussions about how the brain works. There are different theories about what these parts do to affect how an athlete performs. Why is the brain separated into two hemispheres? By having two hemispheres, humans are capable of processing different types of information simultaneously. It's almost like having two brains, but they also share information as well. It also allows you to decipher information quicker. The left side may handle speech, while the right side is providing facial expressions. Most of the movements we perform are directed by the motor cortex located at the back of the frontal lobe. Many of these movement commands will be analyzed and filtered by the cerebellum which sends the information down the spinal cord to the muscles. The cerebellum and the motor cortex of the right side of the brain are responsible for how accurately the muscles in the legs and arms move. There are other parts of the brain that help with movement as well. The brain is interconnected in so many ways that it is imperative to maintain a relaxed state of mind to contribute to the "flow" of information for the movement to be well timed. For example, just to take one step, the eyes see where to go, by sending information from the retina through the optic nerve to the occipital lobe, and there it determines it needs to send this information to the right frontal lobe and motor cortex, which then decides that the legs need to move and consequently sends the information to the cerebellum that coordinates the signals. Then it sends this information through the brain stem, down the spinal cord, and finally through the branches of nerves that trigger the correct muscles to move the legs and arms. The brain can do all this in approximately 1/100 of a second. Just imagine what is required for the player to orchestrate the golf swing?

The left side of the brain mainly controls language, speech, comprehension, writing and some emotions. The left side is more analytical. The right side is more creative. The right brain favors art, music skills, rhythm, visualization, imagination and is responsible for spatial acuity (visual space). **(See FIG. 7)** If you consider the general characteristics of the two sides, it is apparent that the better athlete would need to favor the right brain. As golfers, we tend to analyze our swing and use swing thoughts to make adjustments. This is done by the left brain. The right brain helps the golf swing move more fluidly with visualization, spatial acuity, creativity and imagination. Since information between the two hemispheres is often shared, it is not good to force swing thoughts into the right side because it will produce confusion and tension. Since the right side is the naturally athletic side, it is best not to let the left brain interrupt the train of thought in the right brain. If you can focus on your routine and visualization, you can prevent the unwanted thoughts from getting into the right side. Since the brain is so interconnected, any confusing information sent by the motor cortex and right frontal lobe will tell the cerebellum to send signals that will create poor balance and sudden bursts of energy, causing the muscles to destroy the flow of the swing.

Relating to sports, there is relevance to the left brain, right brain argument. The key point is that the left brain needs to stay out of the way for producing a good golf swing. Another thing about the brain that affects movement is that information can flow back and forth. This is how the brain can be trained. It is capable of making corrections. By performing repetitive drills the brain will alter its thinking to fit the new movements you are trying to accomplish. The left brain does not destroy your swing with swing thoughts. The left merely makes suggestions for the right side to follow. By doing repetitive drills, the swing thoughts will become so entrenched into the thought process of the right side that it will eventually turn into an automatic messaging process. If the messaging is repeated it will improve your ability to duplicate the same motor skills every time you swing the club.

I often stand over a putt questioning if I read the break correctly. ANY doubt will cause you to misdirect the swing, producing a pulled or pushed shot. Why would the brain cause this to happen? Why does doubt create negative side effects? For some reason, the brain sends incorrect signals to our muscles controlling the movement of the club. The cerebellum must send the proper signals, or the result will be an uncoordinated motion. The brain sends messages based on memories from previous motions. When preparing to putt you are combining memories and new information that was formulated in the reasoning analytical part of the brain. This combination of thought is then relayed to the cerebellum. If the new information concerning the break in the putt is not a fully committed message, then other secondary thought signals (optional thinking) are sent to the cerebellum. Thus, you have opposing signals received by the cerebellum, which sends two different signals to the muscles. By reviewing the thinking process, it is clear why

LEFT BRAIN VS. RIGHT BRAIN

FIG. 7

The left brain <u>analyzes</u> the challenges you face on the golf course vs. the right brain, which <u>creates</u> the conditions for how the muscles should move to accomplish your objectives. Your athletic ability is controlled by the right side of the brain.

the putt is not performed accurately.

It is very important to understand this thinking process if you desire to improve. If you mentally know what to avoid while playing, your swing can become more fluid and natural. Only singular messaging should be sent to our muscles. All secondary messages must be avoided. Secondary messages would include negative thoughts, swing thoughts, and doubt.

The next time you prepare to stand over a putt, do you want ONE committed thought being sent to the cerebellum and muscles or do you want TWO uncommitted messages sent? The answer should be clear! This thought process must be used for all shots in golf. If you are not committed mentally to any shot, you are just guessing. Guessing is not the message you want your muscles to receive. I can't emphasize enough how important this rational is for improving your game. How the brain works for preventing unwanted messaging and creating confidence is so important for success in any sport.

You're standing over a difficult pitch shot that must fly over a nearby sand trap and there is little green to work with. You sense the pressure, and unfortunately, you foresee images of the ball landing in the trap. You make several practice swings, follow your normal routine, and you are committed to the shot. Even though there was doubt in your mind, you were able to overcome the uncertainty, and you are committed and ready to swing. But due to added pressure, your muscles are not relaxed, and the swing you finally commit to is stiff and mechanical. Being confident and committed to a shot will not overcome tension. Tension is not always the result of uncertainty. Setting goals and high expectations will produce pressure and tension no different from uncertainty.

When a challenging situation arises, the pituitary gland in the brain sends a message to the adrenal glands that infuse excess cortisol into the bloodstream, which increases blood pressure. As a result, the muscles receive less blood, causing them to tighten. Tight muscles do not promote a smooth golf swing. When swinging the club for a difficult pitch shot, you must be very relaxed. The club must be swung in a structured "care-free" manner. What is a structured "care-free" swing? It is a rehearsed swing wherein the basics of structure of the swing pattern are adhered to, and during the process, you have no concern for the results that will occur. Thinking about results can override the thinking process and create tension. A relaxed "care-free" swing will produce better tempo and timing. Having the skill to not worry about results will allow you to swing with freedom.

There will always be new input information because every shot you attempt on the course is different. The lie, the wind, and the position of the target are always changing. This new information must be sent from the frontal lobe to the cerebellum and then to your muscles. If unnecessary information is relayed, it may "cloud" your thinking. Once you have committed to a shot, only focus on your target, not the ball.

It is well known fact that the brain does not focus well if it must think about more than one thing. So, where should your concentration be focused, the ball or the target? The brain should be focused with your attention being 20% on the ball and 80% on the target, not the other way around! Let's add to this formula and see what happens to our ability to focus properly. If you leave the focus on the ball at 20% and add one swing thought to the mix, your focus will become 40% swing thought, 40% target, and 20% ball. Add one negative thought to this mixture and the situation is compounded. The target now takes a "back seat" and is lost in the formula for a good golf shot: 40% swing thought, 40% negative thought, 20% ball, and 0% target. If you consider this seriously, you realize how important a clear functioning mind is required for success on the course.

In the following chapters I discuss methods for improving the mental approach to golf. I will also diagnose what the greatest players did differently to achieve their ultimate success.

Chapter 2
Visualization

"I never missed a putt in my mind"

Jack Nicklaus

Golf is a sport that incorporates being idle most of the time, but while playing other sports there is continuous action. There is little time in most sports to contemplate how you will need to move your body to accomplish a desired result. With sports like football or basketball, a previously rehearsed play is performed on the field or court, and the players go through the motions to catch a ball or shoot a basket. In both cases the action is so quick that there is little time to think about it. You simply react at that moment to accomplish a feat.

In golf, there is a great amount of time for contemplation before striking the ball. This extra time is a real issue in golf. With the added time to contemplate the shot you are about to perform, the game becomes a sport wherein "it's all mental". It not that deliberation is detrimental to the golf swing, it's just that the amount of time to deliberate is too long. Concentration can be good if all your thinking is positive. However, with all that time on your hands between shots, it is not uncommon for a negative thought to creep into your mind. This is the crux of the problem with golf. It's almost unavoidable. How the time between shots is used will often determine the success of a golfer. If you can control your mind by only thinking positive thoughts, you will have conquered a major hurdle in golf. I often refer to Ben Hogan for making a point. He was so focused he rarely spoke to anyone between shots. He knew that if he were in the right frame of mind, he could always produce the shot he desired. All the greatest golfers know how to use this time between shots, and achieve the best results. Some players were the opposite of Hogan. Lee Trevino loved to talk all the time between holes. But when it came time to concentrate, he did it as well as any great golfer. The point is that the time between shots must include only positive thinking. You must find a way to block out negative thoughts.

After arriving at the ball, this is what separates the better players. If, by chance there are further delays caused by outside influences, such as another player has hit their ball into the woods and they are looking for their ball, or the group ahead is playing too slow, you must maintain a calm demeanor and not let your mind wander. At the sight of the ball, it is all about being focused.

When it's time to pull the trigger for the shot at hand, there are two words that describe the circumstances: Contemplation and anticipation. As the player contemplates the shot at hand, too often there is so much opportunity to speculate what could happen if something is done incorrectly. That would include; incorrect aim, improperly judging distance, or poor execution of the swing. If your mind is thinking about every possibility before starting the swing, the results are already determined. Your mind must be focused only on the situation at hand. There can be no conjecture, which produces uncertainty and tension. Focus must be on the anticipation of making a great shot to the predetermined target. It is so important to conceive how this can affect your game. In the Foreword section of the book, I mentioned the ability to tap-in a short putt with little or no thought. I believe there is an answer to how this action can occur. The word that describes this casual motion is "anticipation".

Anticipation is a glance into the future. It is similar to visualization. The only difference between the two is that visualization is pre-planned and anticipation is spontaneous. It is predicting a good outcome before it happens. The brain is capable of so many special abilities, including what could be called premonition. When casually tapping in a three-foot putt, you are foreseeing the ball go into the hole just a split second before striking the ball. Anticipation is the key to making more putts. Anticipation is a target oriented swing. It is a natural feel that is the result of the eyes glimpsing at the target, and then the body spontaneously orients itself to complete the task. I will call this, "the magic move". Anticipation will work with the full swing as well. If you can imagine your hands reaching toward the target as you hear contact. Your mental focus is ahead of the impact. The mind is anticipating the target. The mind must imagine the flight of the ball as your hands move out in front of you. It's time to turn imagination into something real. Do not be fixated on how you swing. Instead focus on what you anticipate will happen and then let the body and club just move to complete the pattern. Golf needs to become more about anticipation and less about the past and present.

Too much thinking in golf is backward, not forward. The past cannot be changed. What is done is done! If you are always ahead of the ball instead of behind, you will make great shots. All your bad shots will no longer be in your rearview mirror if you are forward-thinking. The anticipation of what will happen will block out the past. Seeing the ball leave the tee before the club arrives for impact will direct the movement of your body in how you practiced beforehand. You are letting the brain direct the swing in a way that is automatic, not controlled by thinking. This process uses some of the brain that we have not been using to full capacity. Seeing a future event in your mind a split second before it occurs is the secret to playing better golf. All great players in every sport are doing this when they are "in the zone". Analysts have often used this phrase, and this is the best way to explain the mental process. By looking forward you are predicting the outcome, and the cerebellum in the brain just makes the muscles move to follow the forethought that was imagined in the frontal lobe section of the brain. Basically, our imagination is controlling muscles, which is "the magic move". To be "in the zone" is all about forward-thinking.

Is there a way to train your mind to think ahead, instead of now? Amateurs often use the other option, "thinking in the past". The right hemisphere of the brain can play a role in this forward thinking since this part of the brain is associated with creativity, imagination, and spatial surroundings. Thusly, the right side of the brain is the side that great athletes use more so than the left. The only way to answer the previous question is, to practice visualization. Visualization is the key for learning forward-thinking.

Visualization is similar to anticipation. Both require a form of imagination. Learning to create a movie in your mind may be the best way to improve your game without a lot of physical effort. The beginning of your setup routine is the best time to visualize the target in your mind. You will need to practice visualization before using it on the course. Start first at home, thinking about a good routine you want to use for setup. Have a definite plan which includes standing behind the ball and choosing a target a few feet in front of the ball that aligns with the distant target. Then, set up to the ball by aligning the clubface and body to the nearby target spot. Once the alignment is complete, look to the target and be sure to pick out a detailed target, look back to the ball, waggle the club a couple times, look again at the distant target, take a "snapshot" of the target, return your eyes to the ball area, think target, and start the swing. Imagine the movie you made in your mind and repeat this several times until you have it memorized.

In addition to learning a routine you are learning how to visualize. In order to better secure the snapshot of the target, practice this visualization technique on the range. Look at the yard marker at the range as you setup. Now imagine your eyelids as a shutter and take a picture of the yard marker you have targeted. Plant the image in your mind, then focus on the ball for a second and start the takeaway. Be sure the picture is clear in your mind, in full color, not black and white. At this point do not attempt to visualize a movie of the balls flight. It's a snapshot. Once this is rehearsed many times, then you can play a movie as you swing the club. Do not rush the process. The snapshot must be a strong image, so the glance back to the ball will not over-shadow the target image in your mind.

After the routine is memorized, do the same for the full swing. Imagine performing the entire swing in slow motion and include details of certain parts of the swing you may be working on. Start the movie with the takeaway, cocking the wrists, completing the backswing, shifting left during transition, maintaining wrist angles coming down, releasing the club, contacting the ball, full extension follow-through, and finish with a pose. Repeat this movie in your mind until you have memorized every detail. Then do both the routine setup and swing at full speed. When you do the swing recall at full speed, try to view this as a movie with no swing thoughts. Try to view as if you were watching a professional golfer on TV. Eventually add the flight of the ball to the target and your movie is now complete. Finally edit your movie for deciding what you want to use for the routine for the course. **(See FIG. 8)**

Jack Nicklaus has spoken about the importance of visualization for the golf swing. In his book, "Golf My Way", he suggests that this was one thing he did so well that it was the main reason for his success. He said he could see the ball being struck, fly through the air and land at the target, all before he started the swing. He said he created a movie in his mind and just completed the swing with the movie in the back of his mind. Many have suggested that Jack Nicklaus may be the best golfer of all time, so why not follow his statement that visualization was the key to his success.

You have a particular hole on the course you play, and for some unknown reason, it has become your nemesis

VISUALIZATION

FIG. 8

Start a routine by picturing in your mind every detail of the target you have chosen. Visualize a movie of the ball flying in the air and landing at the target.See the movie again as you start the swing.

hole. Every time you play it, you hit a bad shot. You may even speculate before your day started, thinking what can I do to prevent the inevitable. This is when a good routine and the use of visualization could produce different results. Visualization is your way of anticipating a good shot before contact is made. It's a method of creating a preferred future event. Just like the one-handed tap-in, your brain controls your body to spontaneously do things that may seem nearly impossible.

Visualization plays a major role in developing a good setup routine. A routine must flow like water moving in a stream. If your routine has rhythm it will encourage your swing to have a smooth tempo. In other words, the tempo of your setup will affect the timing of your swing. The basal ganglia in your brain, is responsible for rhythm. Therefore, if you want to perform something involving rhythm better, you will need to train this part of the brain with an organized method of practice. Repeating a routine will produce better results.

We all have some routine in our lives and most of the time we don't think about it. In golf, your setup should become so automatic that it just happens. As humans, we love routine because it makes us feel calm and allows us to escape from the normal activities that can often create stress. If you want to have a relaxed golf swing, this is the answer.

I have a 12 foot mat I setup on my back patio to work on my putting stroke. Part of the mat has a wedge of foam on the backside. This provides a hole for the ball to drop into. Every time I make a putt, I pull the ball out of the hole with the end of the putter. The putter has a small-sized mallet head and the toe is rounded. After pulling the ball out I always take the rounded toe end of the clubhead, and I casually hit the ball about 10 feet to hit the ball again. One day, I thought to myself, how is it I can hit this small round ball with the rounded tip of my putter and make it go where I choose? A round tip hitting a round ball should be near impossible, but my mind spontaneously directed my arm and hand to do this action nearly accurate every time. I have often seen some of the professionals do this action with their putter when their ball lies in thick grass just off the green. How can our brain help us accomplish such difficult feats?

This scenario may seem trivial, but it got me to thinking about just what is possible as we search to understand ways to harness these extraordinary skills. Maybe the two greatest golfers of all time discovered how to use these skills. For Hogan it was the repetitive training and for Nicklaus it was visualization. What other skills can we add to the list? If we can tap into some of what the brain is truly capable of, we might see amazing results. This advanced skill could be how to improve visualization. The next level would be the art of anticipation. The reason I was able to strike the ball accurately with the rounded tip of the putter was because my mind foresaw the future event of the predicted landing spot (the target). If you have total commitment to ONLY the target, the mind and body produce the desired results, which in this case, was the unimaginable feat of accurately hitting a round ball with a round instrument. As long as you are thinking forward, you will not be harboring any negative thoughts. Projective thinking will help direct future events. A word of caution, you must not think ahead too far. You cannot think about results. Results happen, but they should not be your primary goal. You are simply "wishing" the ball to reach its target. If you use wishful thinking on every hole, your game will definitely improve.

Visualization may be the best way to train the brain to perform actions that are beyond the norm. It can allow us to use some of the brain we don't normally use for playing golf. As I mentioned earlier, this was a special talent for Jack Nicklaus. He could have won over 30 major championships, considering he finished second 19 times. Still, 18 is a record that may never be broken. We must listen to the best golfers in the world if you want to improve your game. Jack did not try to hide a secret like Ben Hogan. He possessed something as special, if not more special than Hogan's secret. Considering Jack's success, he may have captured the greatest secret of all for golf.

The one thing that stands out in his illustrious career is how Jack used visualization better than any golfer during the time he was at the top of his game. With his record he may have taken the art of visualization to a different level. As I said previously, he could visualize a movie before the shot, as well as, play back the movie in his mind during the shot. This encouraged body movements to follow the picture in his mind to produce the ideal shot. This is what is different about Jack's use of visualization. His mental approach to golf may have been the best to ever play the game!

To help with his visualization process, he also used "self-talk". This is simply, talking softly to yourself describing the shot you want to play. This is not that uncommon among many of the great players. This will increase the clarity of the planned shot and it will eliminate the opportunity for the brain to be confronted with unwanted negative thoughts. These lyrics combined with visual effects will create a complete movie of the entire shot, which includes seeing the ball fly to the intended target. Jack would go one step further, not only seeing the landing spot on the green, but also foreseeing the next shot of the putt going into the hole. This is what greatness is about.

Earlier I discussed how to use anticipation as the next level of visualization. This is what Jack Nicklaus was doing by foreseeing future events in his mind. This may be the secret for better golf that is not being taught by most golf instructors. If you want to get to the next level in golf, find a golf instructor that includes visualization as part of their teaching program.

A little more thought concerning anticipation. The better you become at anticipation, the body will make adjustments to correct something without our thinking about it. What is happening, you are using anticipation to let the brain direct the swing in a way that is automatic, not controlled by thinking. As fast as the thought process may be, it is not as fast as looking forward, before the move occurs. This thinking process uses some of the brain's capacity that is not often used. Forecasting a future event is the secret for playing better golf.

Since the target is not the ball, how can the golfer see a target without looking at it? Previously, I discussed different ways to learn how to visualize. If you want to take visualization to the next level you must practice swinging with your eyes closed. I recommend doing the practice sessions on the range with very few people around. Occasionally, you will strike a mishit shot. The goal is only to develop a pure form of visualization.

Start by closing your eyes for putting and chipping. Look at the target and memorize the direction and distance. Close your eyes and make two or three practice swings. Picture the target in your mind and feel the shot. Next, peek for a second to move into your setup position. Then close your eyes and visualize the memorized picture in your mind and swing. Do this over and over until the ball stops near the target almost every time. Do not change the target. Stay in the same position and now do the same process but swing with your eyes open every other shot. Continue making practice swings with your eyes closed. Do not deviate from the routine of every other shot. Next, increase the distance by 50%. If you started at 10 feet, move back to 15 feet. If you were chipping from 10 yards, move back to 15 yards. Use the same club for chipping. Repeat the entire process. Look at the target with eyes open and memorize the picture of the target, make two or three practice swings with eyes closed, and swing with eyes closed. Eventually you can again alternate swings with eyes closed, then with eyes open. I repeated these instructions again because it is important not to rush the process. Do not try swinging with eyes open every shot. Wait another day or two before opening your eyes more often. This is the process I used to eliminate the yips, and it does work. To my surprise, I discovered that I was learning the process of visualization and was not immediately aware how this method of training was the best way to accomplish this feat. It does not matter what level you are in golf. This will improve your ability to visualize better than other methods often suggested by swing coaches.

Closing your eyes eliminates distractions you were not even aware of with previous training methods. Our eyes control so much of how we perform. Some of what the eyes see can be distractions to pure thinking. With the eyes closed the memories in our brain will be more vivid without the interruptions from the outside world. Swinging with eyes closed provides the purest thinking you can achieve. If you can establish this pattern of thinking well enough, you will eventually be able to duplicate this process with your eyes open. After you have reached this ultimate level of performance, you may still choose to keep your eyes closed for your practice swings.

Will this concept work with the full swing? As I said earlier, you may want to be in an open area of the range, especially as you begin with your eyes closed while swinging. Start with the pitching wedge and work your way up. If you normally hit your pitching wedge 130-140 yards, locate a target on the range near this distance. Start by focusing intently on your target. Next, close your eyes and make two or three practice swings thinking solely on the target you memorized in your mind. You may need more practice swings at first to establish more feel for the shot you are picturing. When you make the practice swings, you want the target to be more vivid in your mind than what you first viewed with your eyes open. When you step forward to setup to the ball, just peek momentarily to establish a position. This must be done with little delay, then with your eyes closed, return to the picture in your mind and swing. To help this process flow freely, it is best to tee several balls about 6 inches apart in front of you. This will allow you to focus on process rather than distractions.(See FIG. 9)Follow the same format you used for putting and chipping. Do not rush to start swinging every other shot with the eyes open. You must develop an extreme feel for each shot before progressing. Do not change to a different club and target until your accuracy is beyond anything you have previously experienced.

After you have practiced this concept with several clubs and different targets, you should be able to visualize better than you ever thought possible. At that point, you will need to develop your setup routine that will include some of the patterns you used with your practice sessions. For a while you may want to continue the practice swings with your eyes closed, unless you feel you have fully acquired the visualization clarity you need for success on the course. The purpose of doing all these drills is to find a way to eliminate all the distractions that often occur when your eyes are open.

MULTI-BALL LINEUP

FIG. 9

By lining up 5 or more balls at the range, you can swing with the same freedom as your practice swing. This is an ideal method for establishing tempo and timing. Use the same line-up for the close your eyes drill, which is recommended as the best method for learning the art of visualization.

Your goal is to have a more vivid image of the target. After you have used this visualization technique for a while on the course, it's time to try something beyond the norm. A step above visualization is anticipation. Jack Nicklaus used this process, but it didn't have a name. It was his way of perfecting the visualization process. What Jack did was similar to calling a shot in pool. In pool, you might say, "Eight ball, bank shot into the side pocket". You are projecting a future event. If you are a good pool player, you visualize how to aim, and you see the shot happen before you start moving the cue-stick. So how does this compare to golf. Jack would often self-talk describing how he would setup, predict the swing method, predict the flight of the ball, forecast the landing area, and then forecast the shot that was to follow. All this before the "now" shot was attempted. Why is this significant? Planning ahead encourages the mind to excel in establishing confidence and improving performance. Extreme confidence blended with vivid visualization will produce the ultimate level of success.

All people use anticipation to make decisions. Every major decision you ever made was done by considering the pros and cons, or "what-ifs". The brain has the ability to forecast the future based on memories and experiences. You could call this action, "common sense predictions". Just like the pool player, the golfer has the ability to predict the shot about to be struck, and the following shot if they put themselves in the proper position.

There are two types of anticipation. The first is immediate, and the second is projected. Immediate anticipation, I discussed earlier, is when you are casually tapping in a putt. You literally see the ball falling into the hole just as you make contact. This occurs because your main focus was the hole. The ball simply got in the way of the club path. The eyes saw the hole and the brain perceived the hole as the only target. The ball could have been an egg. The brain didn't care, since the only focus was the hole. A golfer that backhands a two-foot putt into the hole doesn't remember contacting the ball because they anticipated the ball going into the hole just before it was struck. Golfers could perform in this manner for longer putts, if they let the brain perform the target oriented motions. Instead, we try to control what the brain does naturally. It is difficult for all humans to let go of the desire to be in control. We all tend to over-think what should be a more natural process. The other extreme is that you don't care, wherein you say, "It doesn't matter whatever happens. I don't care about the outcome." Where do you need to be to perform your best? Actually your mental approach should be closer to "I don't care what happens". Of course, this mental approach is too extreme. The mental state for playing golf should be "whatever happens, just happens". Golf should be played with casual control. You use your skill to the best of your ability, but in the end, "whatever happens, just happens". This is what the brain is thinking when the casual backhand motion is used to tap in the short putt. For this, little skill was required because the brain just reacts based on previous experiences of a similar situation, in this case, previous tap-ins.

When the brain is performing a skill solely based on past experiences, it can perform unimaginable feats, especially when there are no distractions. If your mind is clearly focused on the target, the mind will send the appropriate signals to the cerebellum and the rest of the body. Your mind is occupied with visual projections of the shot to be attempted, such that the body will naturally respond to produce the best results based upon your skill level.

The other form of anticipation is projected anticipation. This is what was previously discussed when Jack Nicklaus was predicting a shot ahead of the shot being attempted. Comparing golf to pool is a good way to play golf. All golfers should play for position to make the next shot easier to perform. This is especially true for approach shots to a green. If you can place the ball in a position for an uphill putt, your odds are greater for making the putt that follows. The pros try to do this all the time because they prefer uphill putts. The slope of the green should determine where you want your ball to land for an easier putt that is to follow. Most greens are sloped toward the fairway for drainage. This is why the pros are normally short rather than long in their approach shot to the green. You may think they should be playing an extra club, but the real reason is they are planning ahead for an uphill putt. This concept of planning ahead can save many strokes during a round of golf. If you are good at pool, you can relate to the importance of positioning the ball for an easier NEXT shot.

Chapter 3
Better Focus

"For this game you need above all things, to be in a tranquil state of mind."

Harry Vardon

When the golfer prepares to make a shot, they focus on the ball and a target. How do our brains function to accomplish this effort of concentration? First, you make visual contact. The message goes through the optic nerve to the occipital lobe located in the back of the brain, which instantaneously sends a message to the prefrontal lobe in the front of the brain. Coincidentally the area in the frontal lobe is located just behind the eyes. As I described earlier, synapses are located just outside the neurons. These synapses have little sacs of chemicals that are sometimes released to connect the gap between the connectors. These chemical connections make it possible for neurotransmitters to carry information through axons to other neurons. There are certain chemicals in the brain that produce different results. The chemicals involved for focusing intently are a combination of acetylcholine and dopamine. The chemicals will help determine the type of message that is sent to make the focus process happen.

For some reason, some golfers have the ability to focus more intently than others. Obviously, it would require more neurons and neurotransmitters to make this happen. So how does the average person increase this activity in the brain? There are ways to train the brain to improve focus. Like anything, if you want to improve something you have to practice, which is done with repetition. Psychologists recommend playing video games, chess, and puzzles for improving focus. In addition, any activities that involve targeted focus, such as darts, cornhole, pool, and gun range.

The brain must be trained no differently than training your body.

Trying to improve focus will not matter if you don't know what to focus on when you are about ready to start your swing. Previously, I provided details about the brain function involved in the focusing process, and it is clear that intense focus is more than visual. Visual focus has different connections in our brain that include emotions as well. This is what determines the intensity of focus between different players. How we control our emotions will affect how well we concentrate. This combination may dictate how well a golfer can focus on a target. Also, if this process is interrupted with swing thoughts or negative thoughts this information flow will be interrupted resulting in loss of focus.

Since golf provides an extraordinary amount of time before the swing begins, focusing should be preformed better than with any other sport. But, for some reason, this extra time is not used properly for good focus. In hockey, the players are focusing only for a split second for striking the puck and they are almost always able to hit the puck where planned. The delay to strike a golf ball is so long compared to other sports that it is difficult to maintain focus. The brain cannot stay focused long enough to continue the flow of information. The real problem is that the ball is not the main target, so the focusing process for golf must also involve the use of visualization.

There can be no better time to suggest a humorous reflection. The movie "Happy Gilmore" was a true classic.

"Happy" would take just a second to stand behind the ball, then run forward and strike the ball immediately without any preparation. Since the storyline is based on a hockey player turned golfer, this is a technique you might expect. In reality, this method of play could be a better way. I am not sure when the tradition of a long routine to start the swing actually got started. I am sure that in the early history of golf this long period of deliberation was not part of the process. Back then, golfers likely stepped into position and hit the ball with little delay, not that different from "Happy Gilmore". All sports have evolved over the years. It is my opinion, golf took a wrong turn. If golf were played without this considerable delay just for contemplating a shot, I believe the sport would be more enjoyable. Possibly, there is a "Happy Gilmore" out there that could prove my point.

If you watch the pros on TV, this preparation time before the swing has actually become longer than it was 50 years ago. Palmer and Nicklaus definitely had a shorter routine. Amateurs have a tendency to follow what the pros are doing. Some of this cause for delay has to fall on the backs of golf instructors. The younger golfers start out swinging almost immediately when they set up to the ball. For some reason, they eventually acquire this unnecessary long delay from instructors and pro golfers. I have to admit that I have become part of this trend. I am not sure why golfers now take so much time between observing the target and starting the swing. A golfer will perform better by shortening this focusing time. Unfortunately, habits are hard to break. It requires retraining the brain to follow a different rhythm. Unlike the hockey player, with the extra time the golfer must learn how to focus more intently to recall the target image. This extended time for focus will normally produce tension.

Most amateurs use this delay for letting the left part of the brain review swing thoughts. Since the natural thought pattern is interrupted, the swing will become segmented and out of sync. This can be resolved by reducing the time in your setup routine by as much as 30-50%. Is this possible without destroying your swing? I can guarantee it is. In all likelihood, we could swing like Happy Gilmore and probably play better than we do now. Practice the shorter delay by looking at the target and mentally take a snapshot of a specific target, look back to the ball, visualize the image of the target, and swing.

When focusing, do not become fixated on the ball. Focus on the entire ball rather than a spot or dimple. If someone throws a ball toward you, what do you focus on when you attempt to catch it? You see the whole ball, not a part of the ball. When setting up to a golf ball and your focus is on a small marking, you will be thinking only about the ball as your target. If you were preparing to throw a dart to a dart board, would you be looking at the dart the entire time? If you did, you would likely miss the entire board when you threw the dart. When you instruct your mind to focus on something very specific that will become your primary target. Granted, you have some focus dedicated to your secondary target (the ball), but it cannot be so intense that the primary target, a spot on the fairway or green is lost in your conscious mind. If you <u>think</u> about the primary target, you will see the ball as a blurred white circle and it just gets in the way of the passing clubhead as you swing.

What you are trying to accomplish is very similar to what the hockey player does when striking a puck. The golf swing should become a more natural process with little delay after viewing the target. Unlike playing darts, where you can stare at the target during the entire process, golf can only be done by creating a visual image of the primary target, while focusing on a secondary target. Learning how to retain the mental focus of the primary target, while not looking at it, is essential for better golf.

Your setup routine can still be well planned, but once you are aligned and feel relaxed, the remaining process should be less than 4 to 5 seconds. It is okay to look at your target more than once during the setup routine. This is the time you need to get settled and aligned. All golfers should use a target spot a few feet in front of the ball just for establishing proper alignment. The distant target is too far away for your setup to be accurate. The last look at the target is when you take your snapshot. So you can retain this picture, there can be little delay before starting your swing once you look back to the ball. The glance back to the ball should only allow time for proper breathing.

Breathing must be part of the focusing and part of your routine. So what is recommended for breathing when you are preparing to swing? There is no clear "set in stone" method for breathing during the routine. Deep breathing will help maintain a relaxed mind and body. It is a good idea to take a deep breath when you stand behind the ball at the beginning of the routine. This is the signal to your mind: "It's time to start the focusing process". It will start your routine with a sense of relaxation. After this deeper breath, then breathe normally, but not shallow. Be sure your jaw and face are relaxed. Your golf instructor will always suggest this relaxation region, because this is where tension starts.

The question that is often asked, how do I breathe the second before the swing starts? This is a personal matter. There are recommended ways to breath at this point, but it still comes down to what feels right for you. There are two theories on this. Some instructors will suggest breathing in during the backswing and breathing out during the downswing. This can be difficult unless you have a very slow swing. If the swing is approximately one second from takeaway to impact, this would not be a relaxed breathing technique. The other option is to take your last deep breath just as you take your last look at the target and then start to let it out as you look back to the ball. You will have some remaining breath to exhale as you start the backswing. The exhale can be your trigger to start the swing. Just remember, breathing is one of the best methods to achieve relaxation. Be sure a breathing pattern is part of your routine. Breathing can be the instrument for establishing a cadence or tempo during setup.

Relaxation is so important for the entire game of golf. It will affect putting and chipping even more than the full swing. Again, be sure your jaw is relaxed throughout the entire swing. In the past, when swinging a driver or 3 wood, I would occasionally grit my teeth at the start of the downswing. Almost every time I did this, I would hook the ball far to the left. "If you can keep a smile on your face while swinging, you will have a smile on your face after you hit the ball!"

Relaxation is only possible if the brain does not sense something stressful. The hypothalamus near the center of the brain receives signals from the frontal lobe when witnessing something that you determine to be an undesirable situation. The hypothalamus transmits this information to the nearby pituitary gland. The pituitary gland is very small, about the size of a pea. It can control emotions by sending information to the adrenal glands, located just above the kidneys. The adrenal glands release hormones which can affect heart rate, blood pressure, and blood sugar levels. The hormone(s) will produce stress when these levels become elevated. The release of the hormone, cortisol, will change how your body functions including stress and tension. If you feel stress on the golf course, you will experience these unwanted side effects. On the other hand, if you are relaxed and experience joy and pleasure, the brain itself is responsible for these feelings. The brain uses different chemicals to transfer a certain type of message. Joy and pleasure are the result of the frontal lobe portion of the brain transmitting information via the release of the chemical dopamine through synapse connections. Various connections then send the information to the amygdala, which is the center that releases the chemical dopamine into the bloodstream.

Maintaining the proper state of mind for golf will greatly affect how you play. Do you play better when you feel stress or when you feel happy? This is not a difficult question? Somehow we get so involved in a sport and we desire only to become a better athlete rather than playing the sport for enjoyment. We create our own stress by setting and seeking unreasonable goals. The focus for golf should involve setting short range goals and then, build on each level.

Occasionally I have gone to a place that I have been to hundreds of times, and suddenly I look in a certain direction and I see something I never noticed before. I asked myself, "How did I not see this until now"? The brain did see this object previously, but it was not important enough at the time, so it discarded its existence. Our brains have memory cells, called engram cells. The engram cells include recent memories and forgotten memories. The forgotten memories can sometimes be reactivated and the memory returns to your conscious mind. Some memories may never be reactivated and are lost forever. Neuorologist are not sure what stimulates the engram neurons to restore an old memory. Because the brain is always producing new memories, it has a way of hiding old memories so that new information is given priority for better recall.

So this particular time I see the object because I am in a very calm state of mind, which made me more aware of the surroundings. These are the times when, you smell the roses, see the birds, and see all that nature has to offer. It's a different feeling than your normally stressful day, filled with distractions. Our brain does not function effectively if we have anything that deprives us of a calm demeanor. If you desire for your brain to function at a higher level, you need to find a way to escape the complex world and focus on a calm and peaceful setting.

This is another important matter to consider for golf. Our brain does not function as well if we are not in a relaxed state of mind. If you want your brain to perform at a level near 100%, you must find a way to escape the complex world for better focus. A relaxed state of mind is your best friend on the golf course. When you possess this calmness, you can play golf like you don't have a care in the world. You can't wait to hit your next shot. If you have no stress while playing, your confidence will soar. So how do you acquire this mental state of absolute calm? This may be the greatest challenge in golf. The only way to accomplish this is to eliminate all thoughts about results. Having a specific rhythmic routine will help, but most importantly, you must not think about results. It is okay to think about a landing spot, but you must not think about what happens if you miss your target. Anticipating a landing spot is different from worrying about the outcome. In other words, you can anticipate a target but you cannot visualize negative outcome. Do your normal routine, and focus on breathing and the target. You are only thinking about the target and your effortless swing will take you there.

When you have this calm state of mind you will have better tempo and timing. When these two facets of your swing are near their best, the swing becomes automatic. The brain will be more aware of your surroundings and function with more acuity. The brain needs to "feel nature around you" when you swing.

Deeper focus typically requires eye contact. Can you focus on a target without eye contact? In golf, you can only "think" about the target. Can other senses improve focus? If you can include other senses in golf, you will definitely improve your mental focus. In addition to your eyes, you also use a sense of touch when golfing. How you softly grip the club will accentuate a feel for the shot you make. Touch can also sense gravity and the weight of the club. Your hands are the only connection to the tool you use to strike the ball. This sense of touch is therefore very important. Hearing can also add to your ability to focus. By sensing the ground beneath your feet and nature surrounding you on the golf course, it increases your sensitivity of awareness for better focus. You can hear the sound of the grass as you walk; you can hear the sound of the club as it whips through the air; you can hear the sound of impact as the ball is struck; and you can hear the wind in the trees and the birds singing. All these sounds should be included in your mind as you focus on your game. Combining all these senses will intensify your mental focus. All these senses are the product of sensitive nerves that communicate back and forth with the brain to accentuate your mental acuity. These nerves are interconnected to the muscles, joints, blood vessels, and organs. Therefore, your nerve center can in some ways communicate with all the body parts and this can greatly intensify your ability to focus. Martial arts incorporates this same type of thinking for maintaining well-being.

One of the biggest enemies in golf is tension. Being a little nervous can actually help you play golf because it does increase adrenaline in your system and this can sharper your skills. However, if being nervous becomes too intense then tension sets in, and this can destroy your game. As a result muscles tighten, heart rate increases, and blood pressure rises. Excessive tension will destroy your ability to focus.

Certain sports like archery, shooting a gun, pool, and darts require intense focus. You may even stare at the target for several seconds before committing to an action. What you are doing with your body and mind to pursue the best results? Your eyes intensely focus on the target. Your mind recalls previous memories of the position of the body and arms to accomplish the task. Once your body is set in an acceptable position, your mind sends the chosen information to the cerebellum to turn these committed thoughts into action. **(See FIG. 10)** We all have participated in some of these sports, and you recall how focused you were to hit the target. Why can't we use this same intense focus in golf? We can. We need to be committed only to the target and let the body determine your actions for more accurate results. In golf, there are two things that prevent this from happening. There is too much body motion to complete the task and there are two targets instead of one. Since the brain is not good at multitasking we need to simplify the body motion and think of one target. But, you must ask, "how do I eliminate either of the targets to focus intently?" This is the

BETTER FOCUS

FIG. 10

Many activities require extreme focus. Add this same intensity to your concentration for golf. Recall the deep thought you devoted to "hit" your target for other sports. Let the target determine your thinking and the body will perform the task.

conundrum in golf! Golf may be the only sport wherein you look at a different target than the one you should be focusing on. Hockey has some of these characteristics, but the primary target is much closer. To score or pass the puck is normally 10 yards away, not 300 yards! So, how do you get around this targeting problem? **(See FIG. 11)**

I have seen golfers putt while looking at the hole. Jordan Spieth has done this successfully, but he will not look at the hole for long putts. I have chipped the ball with my eyes closed and done fairly well. The problem is that the body can't be moving excessively to accomplish this task accurately. Balance enters into the picture when the body has to move a considerable amount. We call this eye-hand coordination. We need our eyes to help control the club path as we move our bodies. I found that chipping with your eyes closed sometimes created uncertainty with the movement of the club. Without the eyes seeing the club move, there can be problems with consistency. For chipping, there is little movement so with a lot of practice you might avoid some of this inconsistency.

It is amazing how much our eyes control muscle movement and balance. This is why we look at the ball instead of the primary target in golf. Since the eyes must look at the ball, the only way to see the other target is to imagine its existence. Here lies the real problem. How do you make the target you are imagining in your mind more vivid than the ball you are looking at while you swing? This is why golf is a difficult sport! As I just laid out, this is not how the brain operates at its best. This is not how our mind

HOW TO FOCUS

"Focus on the flight of the ball before the swing."

During setup, focus on the ball as a place to rest your eyes, while the mind foresees the ball flying to the target.

FIG. 11

and body function as a unit. This leaves us with only one solution, we must learn to intensely visualize in our minds a target we do not see with our eyes. Unfortunately, this is the only way.

Focusing and visualizing are not the same, but they are dependent on each other. Focus is both visual and mental, whereas, to visualize is solely mental and it is more dependent on memory. Obviously good focus involves mainly the eyes, but I believe we are overlooking the mental side of good focus. My son is a Black Belt in Taekwondo. I was fortunate enough to watch his performance for certification before a 10 Degree Black Belt. Receiving a Black Belt in any martial arts is a major accomplishment. The training is far more intense than any sport. After my son's exceptional performance, he received his Black Belt certification from the Grandmaster. Utmost mental focus is required for mastering the control of body movement. So much can be learned from this art to understand how we can focus our minds with such precision and intensity.

The students of martial arts have taught the mind to control negative thoughts. They concentrate solely on positive feelings and defeat all negative forces. They must possess an unyielding spirit that can conquer any obstacle that might try to stop them from completing their goal. They practice incessantly to obtain strength, endurance, and control. Martial arts focuses on "dan-tien" as a source of energy to improve their performance and well-being.

Since golf is both a physical and mental activity, not unlike martial arts, more attention should be directed toward this art for improving focus. In my previous book "Golf Too Many Swing Thoughts", I suggested how dan-tien should be a part of golf. In golf we call this "our core". The dan-tien is located internally, about 4 inches below the navel. This is our center of gravity and balance. This mental control of balance combines the mind and body into a single spirit. It is a focus point for energy and well-being. By using this force in golf you will better control the balance and coordination of the body around the core. This is especially important for golf since there is so much movement and rotation around this center of gravity.

This part of the game is an area that would help the professional golfer. The modern golf professional has many advisors for maintaining and improving their game, which may include a swing coach, a sports psychologist, a caddie, and a performance coach. What is needed is a consultant in the field of martial arts. Mental management and control is the key to success in today's highly competitive game. Dan-tien is a major factor for producing and maintaining a great golf swing. More attention should be directed toward good balance and communicating with our own body. This includes a better understanding for how gravity and the body function in harmony.

Focus involves many facets. Good focus is not just about using your visual senses. Focus must include the entire body and how it moves during the entire golf swing. The most important part of focus is sensing how your body moves around your core. If you focus on rotation and balance your golf swing will improve greatly. Too much emphasis is often placed on weight shift instead of rotation. Proper rotation will keep your body more centered throughout the swing. Being more centered around your core will create better balance and increase speed naturally. If the backswing is performed by rotating around the core correctly, the downswing becomes a natural process.

Proper rotation will also improve your transition at the top of the swing. The transition in the golf swing is pivotal for every shot you make on the course. The pros are constantly working on transition. This is the part that determines the position at impact. If the transition varies in speed just a small amount, the destination of the ball will be greatly influenced. One area that is overlooked is how the body uses gravity while swinging a club. Gravity is the primary force that our muscles must overcome. If you desire to improve the golf swing, you must learn how to use the forces of gravity in harmony with your swing.

At the top of the swing focus on sensing the weight of the clubhead, and as a result the transition between the backswing and downswing will improve. As the golfer starts to unwind, there is a moment when gravity plays a role in how the weight of the clubhead will resist the change in direction. When the lower body moves left and toward the ground, the upper body and clubhead are resisting this change in direction. As the upper body starts to spring back (unwind), the hands and clubhead sense this pull (force), and for a split second they hesitate (pause) to start the change in direction. This split second of time is valuable to the golfer. If your mind can feel the hands, and the pull of the weight of the clubhead, your brain will send messages to the lower body to start turning around its center core for the release of the stored energy. Another way to describe the change of direction: The force of inertia of the clubhead completing the backswing, resists the pull of the body as it starts to unwind. These opposing forces can often produce a pause at the top of the swing. If the weight shift moving forward is quick, gravity will have less time to effect this change in direction and therefore the pause will not be clearly apparent. A good transition should provide a split second of time when the clubhead feels like it is floating in space. This occurs when the energy of the club's inertia equals the pull of force in the opposite direction. This is the perfect transition. This should be what all golfers desire to attain.

If you think about the downswing starting by using gravity, you will produce a better transition. The weight of the club and arms will fall toward the ground just from the force of gravity. Your muscles would have to do nothing to start the downswing. The key to transition is to use your muscles in harmony with gravity for producing the ideal repeatable golf swing. If you ignore gravity, the golf swing will not be fluid. Fluidity is the result of combining energy and gravity.

Your physical connection to the ground is the other consideration for the ideal transition. Rory McIlroy uses gravity by lowering his body toward the ground to start his downswing. This added move provides more force into the ground, and by using his leg strength he pushes off the ground to provide a surge of power to his swing at just the right moment. This is called the squat move, originally used by Sam Snead in the 1940s and 50s. The ideal golf swing is dependent on many important factors, but if the player does not coordinate their training with the force of gravity it will not reach its full potential. A good golfer must feel the weight of the clubhead as they swing, and sense their body being connected to the force of the ground.

The entire swing should be focused on the dan-tien. This energy force thinking process should include setup, backswing, transition, release, impact and follow-through. If the body and mind are more "center core focused" throughout the swing, you can achieve near perfect tempo and timing. Part of the success of the golf swing is having better communication between the mind and body. Good rotation is produced by maintaining a proper spine position and rotating around the core.

Maintaining your head position is so critical for achieving good rotation. Avoid any swing thoughts that can produce tension. Using the bill of your hat by visually keeping it nearly centered above the ball throughout the swing will keep your head level, and prevent you from raising up too soon. This may be the <u>best solution for eliminating early extension</u>. Previously I recommended no swing thoughts while playing. This swing thought is good to use on the course because it is just about staying generally focused on the secondary target: the ball. It is so important to essentially maintain head position until after impact. The base of your neck is the fulcrum of your swing.

Chapter 4
Playing with Confidence

"A leading difficulty with the average player is that he totally misunderstands what is meant by concentration. He may think he is concentrating hard when he is merely worrying."

Bobby Jones

Playing with confidence is vital for succeeding in any sport. For the professional player, this part of golf will normally determine the winner. Confidence is dependent on how you manage memory more so than how many times you have practiced a shot. Every shot you have ever made is stored somewhere in your memory. I am not talking about muscle memory which is stored in the cerebellum. The larger part of the brain known as the cerebrum is where the past memories are stored. This includes every good shot and every bad shot. This is the crux of the problem. Granted, many shots are so deeply buried in the memory portion of the brain, you may think they are long forgotten. I would say this is true, but for some reason you will often recall a memory you thought was so distant in the past and for some reason, it returns to your memory bank. A player can practice 24/7 for months and now you are playing in a tournament and the game is on the line. You are faced with a difficult chip in thick rough and you have to loft the ball over a sand trap with very little green in front of the pin. You know you can make this shot and it will need to be performed with perfection. After several practice swings, you think to yourself, "I've got this". Then suddenly, just as you are ready to take the club away, a glimpse of a past poorly played shot appears in your mind. Out of nowhere, there it is. But, it's too late. Your club hits to deep behind the ball and the ball lands in the sand trap, making your effort to get down in 2 shots almost impossible. What caused this sudden glimpse of a mishit from the past? Could this have been avoided? How can this negative thought overtake the muscle memory achieved with hours of practice? We still know so little about how the brain works. You would think that the hours of practice and established confidence would supersede any flash of negative thought. Unfortunately, your memories are always there.

This is the battle that must be fought and this is the one part of the brain we need to attempt to control. Stray negative thoughts can affect even the best players in the world. By being consumed with tension and pressure, there is a greater possibility for creating mental uncertainty. You cannot have ultimate confidence if there is just a fraction of doubt. Doubt is simply the by-product of recalling negative thoughts. Even if a group of neurons fire for 1/1000 of a second to release an unwanted memory, all that was rehearsed for years, is destroyed by a split second of doubt. Recalling a past memory may be difficult to prevent, unless you can be proactive in how to stop negative thoughts. We must find a way to prevent any possibility of negative recall that will destroy confidence.

Let's start by revisiting the pitch shot over the bunker. There are only two ways to prevent what I will call, "neuron misfires". I know, this was suggested earlier, but the two solutions are a very structured routine and visualization. Both of these procedures are the "road-blocks" to stop the stray memory neurons from reincarnating. What is being discussed has little to do with what some people call the "yips". The yips is an ongoing issue, not just a single event that may occur occasionally. The yips develop when the misfires occur nearly every time you swing. It is the result of a great number of negative memories, enough to confuse the normally involuntary messages sent from the cerebellum to the muscles in your hands and arms. I will discuss this later in this chapter.

First, let's look at routine to prevent doubt. We all have routines we follow every day. We enjoy sitting down to relax with a cup of coffee every morning. It's how we start our day. We all have certain habits that are common to us. Habits are essentially routines. When we do the same thing over and over it becomes a habit. As the saying goes, "old habits are hard to break". We all love a routine. It seems to put us into a comfort zone. When we are doing these routines in life, it feels like the world around us is just there, and we really don't pay much attention to other things that are happening. It's an escape to our own little world.

If you develop a setup routine for the purpose of escape from your surroundings, you will have taken care of one part of the solution for stopping unwanted thoughts. The routine needs to be just like some of your habits, by going through the motions and not being aware of the procedure. Davis Love Jr. made the following quote, "a routine is not a routine, if you have to think about it". Routines provide a sense of tranquility. All outside influences will no longer affect what is taking place in your mind.

You need to be so entrenched in your routine that the brain will not want to change the status quo. You need to be in your own isolated world, otherwise, the routine is not good enough. Also, a routine is not a routine if you are constantly making changes. Going back to the pitch shot over the bunker. This golfer may have changed the routine by making 5 practice swings instead 3. Or maybe the location for the practice swings was behind the ball instead along the side of the ball. This minor change may have allowed doubt to enter the mind. All this can affect the timing of the swing, which led to "fat" contact with the ball. In addition to the routine, the mind must be focused on the target the entire time. The routine is going on in the background as you visualize the ball landing at the edge of the green and rolling to the hole. This entire procedure is about training your mind, which is just as important as training you body to perform. The training of the mind is no different than the body. Both require repetitive training until your actions become automatic.

The other diversion is visualization. The routine and visualization must be done simultaneously. You create a movie in your mind, seeing the ball land on a targeted spot near or on the green, then foresee it roll out toward the hole. This vivid movie must be playing in your mind as you do the automatic routine. If you are throwing darts at a dartboard and you aim for the bullseye, you let the body position itself without your direction. The positioning of the body is your routine and at the same time, your mind is focused on a movie foreseeing the dart land in the bullseye. I can assure you, if you have ever thrown a dart at a dartboard, you played a movie in your mind of the dart flying to the target and you really never realized it, until now. For almost every sport you play, you have been visualizing by using a movie to improve your skills, and you didn't thought about it. For example, when you throw a football to someone, what is your thought process? You see the person running and you play a movie in your mind to anticipate how far ahead the ball needs to be thrown for their being able to catch the pass. Believe it or not, you produced a movie in your mind to perform this act. For the life of me, I cannot understand why this is not a "staple" in golf, as it is in other sports? All the emphasis in other sports is the target. Where did we go wrong? Somehow the fixation on the golf ball has become the nemesis of golf.

As I discussed in Chapter 2, visualization is as important as how you place your hands on the club. If you practice your swing and use a repeatable routine including visualization, you will develop the confidence to play better golf. This chapter is about confidence and I have mentioned this word only a few times. There is a reason for this. Confidence does not just happen on its own. Having confidence is dependent on how well you have performed an activity in the past. If your chipping game has been bad in the past, you will not be confident every time you setup to the ball. But if you have proper instruction and you have practiced extensively, you should be able to accomplish a skill level near that of a professional. Once you practice something correctly for a significant period of time, the rest of your performance is dependent on mental training.

Some golfers that have near zero confidence will develop the most regretted words in golf, "the yips". I mentioned the cause, but what is the remedy? I experienced this problem several years ago and it is very difficult to overcome. Practice will not solve the problem, which is the usual remedy. The problem lies in the mind, not the body. This issue can only be resolved by retraining the brain. The yips are the result of over-thinking the task at hand. Earlier I discussed the right brain and the left brain. The left brain must not control the swing by creating too many swing thoughts. When your memory adds negative thoughts to the swing thoughts you will create tension and confusion. Confusion will cause the basal ganglia in the center of the brain, which is responsible for rhythm in movement, to send inaccurate signals to the cerebellum and then to the muscles. This will cause the muscles to flinch or tremor just as you are about to strike the ball. This normally happens when chipping or putting because the swing is slow and requires a sense of feel to produce the correct swing pace. Once the brain causes this to occur several times, it will manifest into a habit, and then it becomes nearly impossible to eliminate. At that point, ALL confidence is lost. Many golfers will give up the game because they cannot get rid of the yips.

At one point, I had the yips with chipping and putting at the same time. One day I was practicing at the range, and thought I might try chipping with my eyes closed. I had a good setup position and I kept my left arm straight and my head still, so I figured I would likely be able to strike the ball fairly well with my eyes closed. I pictured the target in my mind and then closed my eyes and thought about the target with my eyes closed, and then completed my swing. To my surprise, my swing was so smooth and free, and after striking the ball I watched the ball land exactly where I pictured. I continued doing this each time I went to the range to practice. Occasionally I would swing with my eyes open. If I failed, I went back to keeping my eyes closed. By randomly swinging with my eyes open I soon established the feel I was looking for. What had happened during this entire process, I learned how to visualize, instead of thinking about swing thoughts and negative memories. Eventually the visualization dominated my swing and I was able to swing with my eyes open all the time. It only took at a few weeks to correct this near impossible problem. I was training the mind to be in charge of my swing. The yips were gone and my confidence returned.

I solved the putting yips by changing my grip to left hand low. Basically I just switched places between the right and left hands on the shaft. This issue took a little more time to correct because changing a grip style can be challenging since the fingers have to find a comfortable position for the grip to feel natural.

After going through this difficult period, I have come to realize how important visualization is for the game of golf. In my opinion, and I am sure many professionals would agree, it may be the secret to becoming a good golfer. All the lessons in the world and all the practice you can manage will not produce the results that are possible with visualization.

The frontal lobe controls our personality and the hypothalamus controls our emotions. Our emotions can affect are self-confidence. If your personality lacks a sense of self-worth, increasing confidence becomes a more difficult task. If our personality can affect how we attain more confidence, we have the chance to improve our effort by becoming a happier person and always think of the glass being half full rather than half empty. If you can have a positive attitude, you can attain positive results. Confidence is built on memories of success. It is easier to achieve confidence if your foundation is stronger to begin with. If you want to train your brain to improve confidence, just remember that negative thoughts will make it harder to accomplish your goal. Confidence is achieved by the mental accumulation of success.

Chapter 5

How to Practice

"There are no shortcuts on the quest for perfection."

Ben Hogan

During the summers in Florida, it can be unbearably hot. The temperature is not majorly hot like Phoenix, but the humidity levels are over 70%. For three straight months the heat index is over 105 degrees. Some people can deal with this heat, but I can't. Therefore, my practice sessions are with or without a club in the back yard or in the house. Basically, I am doing what the northern golfers do in the winter. It's just a different season. If you tee-off early it is sometimes bearable to play here in the summer, but with little or no practicing before the round. During the other three seasons in Florida the weather is ideal for golf. I guess you can't have it all! The bad part about playing in the summer here is going out on the course with little warm up.

How you practice will often determine how you play. The main goal for practicing is to rehearse the correct swing often enough to eliminate thinking on the course. Many parts of the swing should be practiced at home, not on the range. No matter what level of golf you are at, grip, setup, and takeaway should be practiced routinely. These parts of the golf swing should become and remain automatic so that you can concentrate on all the more active parts of the swing. Jack Nicklaus writes in his book, "Golf My Way" that setup and takeaway are the most important parts of the swing. Considering his success, this is a strong statement.

If you are working on something new, it's best to start by doing slow motion drills at home before spending time at the range. It's good to find videos online that will illustrate how to perform a specific move. Locate those golfers that have a similar tempo, so that the changes you are making fit into your swing style and pace. Online you can view both professional golfers and YouTube instructors. If you are an amateur, I would suggest working with instructors that offer the opportunity for you to email videos of your swing, which they analyze and then provide suggestions for correcting any issues. Most of the YouTube instructors break down the swing into parts and all you have to do is request the part that you want to work on and 10 different instructors pop-up online and you are set to go. One problem, most amateurs do not have enough knowledge of the golf swing, so when they try to adjust their swing it often becomes worse. This occurs because the real problem was something totally different from the change they thought was necessary. The golf swing is dependent on all that comes before. If some small thing is done incorrectly in the setup or backswing it will affect all that will follow.

If the professional player has a problem with their swing, they resort to slow motion drills. It's the best way to decipher what you may be doing wrong. It also reinforces the correct move. You will have to do countless repetitions to lock these changes into your mind. You are training the mind to do the same thing time after time. The cerebellum in the brain controls movement and balance. You are cementing these actions into this portion of the brain. It sends these coordinated signals through the spinal cord and then to all the muscles used to make this happen accurately. The more you repeat the action, the more likely the same signals will be sent. If you have a repeatable swing you will be able to perform in a more relaxed state.

When you go to the range always work on one thing at a time. If you are having a difficulty with staying more centered while swinging, spend the entire session on this one thing. If your head is coming up at impact, use a drill just for correcting this and nothing else. The point is, the brain can only fully focus on one thing at a time. It may take several times at the range for one problem to be fixed. It is advisable you work with a golf instructor because you do not want to be practicing the wrong method for any part of the swing. The entire purpose for practicing is to repeat the correct motion over and over so the brain will send the correct signals to the muscles and joints the same way every time.

There are some parts of the swing that require a great deal of attention. Tempo and timing should be rehearsed every time you go to the range. All the new moves you are practicing must be synchronized into the complete swing. If you watch videos of the pros swinging their wedges, it is important to count one, two to establish a feel for their extraordinary rhythm. First start by finding the pro that has a similar swing to your own. By counting, you will soon get a feel for their tempo. Then you can focus on timing. This part of the swing is what I consider to be the biggest difference between amateurs and pros. After breaking down the swing into parts, ultimately this is the most important aspect of the swing to bring everything together. In the end tempo and timing is what determines what type of impact is created. It will determine compression, ball spin, and direction. The only real part of impact remaining is finding the center of the clubface, and I am sure it will affect that as well.

Since tempo and timing are so important, I will discuss these topics in greater detail. How does the mind interact with these facets of the game? First tempo is dependent on your personality type. If you are energetic and hyperactive, you should consider a faster swing tempo. If you are laid back and easy-going, a slower tempo might be your choice. The average professional has a swing ratio of 3 to 1. The downswing to impact is 3 times faster than their backswing. The average pro's downswing is approximately .25 seconds. Thus, the backswing is .75 seconds. This equals one second from start to impact. Follow-through is not part of this equation. I can assure you that the amateur is closer to a 4 to 1 ratio. Even if you choose to use a slower tempo, the swing tempo should not be far from this 3 to 1 ratio. I have a golf watch that provides feedback on swing ratio. I use this almost every time I go to the range. I found that the closer I swing the club to a 3 to 1 ratio, the better my timing, which provides more distance. If I slowed down my backswing and increased the ratio, my results were not as good.

For many years I tried to slow down my backswing, thinking this was a solution to improve timing. I did the opposite of my personality. Instead of slowing down the backswing, I should have increased the speed. If you think slowing down your swing is a solution for poor swing habits you may be mistaken. Your personality must determine your swing tempo. All the years I wasted trying a slower tempo was probably the biggest mistake I made since I started golfing. Several pros have a fast backswing. A good example is John Rahm. He has a short and very fast backswing. I cannot imagine what damage he would do to his game if he slowed down and lengthened his backswing. I am sure he could do this act without major problems, but I can assure you his timing would be greatly affected which would totally change every part of his game.

Every time I go to the range, I observe the amateur golfers. Nearly all amateurs possess a fairly slow backswing. Their normal habit is to take the club back slow and start down fast. The further you move from this 3 to 1 ratio the more likely you will be hitting more shots that hook or slice. Also, it is important not to increase the backswing speed to a point that all the basics are lost. You must be able to finish your body rotation and complete the backswing. Swing tempo should be practiced as often as possible. Once you discover the right tempo, you must reinforce the new rhythm by completing many repetitions.

It is imperative that hand speed before and after the top of the swing closely match. Bobby Jones said his takeaway and the start of the downswing were the same speed. Jack Nicklaus said the speed of the start of the downswing was the same as his speed just before the top of the backswing. These two points are basically the same. Timing the transition at the top of the swing is so critical to creating a good golf swing. This is what separates the pros from the amateurs more than any other issue. Most amateurs move the club slowly to the top, then they increase grip pressure and pull down hard from the top before the lower body has a chance to shift weight to the left side. They are out of balance and normally flip the club through impact.

The brain must be trained properly to match the actions of the professional. Acquiring good tempo and timing is similar to learning a dance move while listening to music. In the "Little Red Book" by Harvey Penick, one of the greatest golf instructors of all time, he tells the story about a student that was continually rushing his swing from the top. In casual conversation during the lesson, Harvey asked the student what he did for a living. The student replied, "I am a dance instructor". Harvey said he laughed and replied to his student. "Your swing is like you are doing the jitter-bug, you should be doing a waltz". From that point on he became one of his best students. This one thought changed his entire thinking for how to swing a golf club. The student could relate to dancing for his new found tempo and improved timing. This is what Harvey did as an instructor. He was a man of few words, but he always knew what to say to influence the "mind" of the student.

How can dancing improve the golf swing? Just like music, dancing involves rhythm. You feel a beat, and the moves for dancing must be smooth and fluid. In dancing you must sequence a pattern of movement. All this is part of tempo and timing. Most dance tempos are 1,2,3 - 1,2,3 - 1,2,3. In golf, you might use this count or just 1,2. Both of these counts can work for timing in golf. The trick is to associate the correct pattern of sequence with the numbers. For example, 1,2,3 – say 1,2 for backswing, 3 for impact.

Timing the numbers is sometimes tricky and you also need to have a certain speed for saying the numbers. I prefer 1,2 – 1 for backswing, 2 for impact. I said earlier that swing thoughts are not good to use while playing on the course. I have found that counting a rhythm is not a swing thought, instead it is a swing feel. Swing feels do not interrupt the flow of the swing.

Mental rhythm can be enhanced by constantly rehearsing tempo and timing. The brain is responsible for creating rhythm. We just need to develop the correct rhythm for golf.

If you feel a lot of tension and you are about to tee off on the first hole, sometimes it is good to let your mind wander and think about things other than golf that make you feel relaxed. Try this on the range to help restore your composure when you are stressed about anything, including your golf game. We all need to escape to a different place just to calm our mind and body. Think about sitting at the beach watching the sunset. Think about a vacation on a cruise ship looking out over the water into the distance and feel the wind in your face. Try this on the range to calm your nerves. If it works for you at the range, you may want to daydream on the golf course when you become stressed and lose confidence in your game.

Even though chipping may be more mental than any other part of the game, there are recommendations for creating consistency. It's best to maintain more weight on the left side, setup with shoulders more level, have an open stance, keep feet close together, and keep your hands slightly ahead of the clubhead at setup and throughout the swing. If you setup properly the remaining challenges for chipping are mental. Some of the mental problems can be resolved by how you time the swing for chipping. Counting while you swing can really improve your timing for the chip shot. Martin Hall suggested this on "School of Golf", the Golf Channel. Counting 1,2,1 is ideal for chipping and it can prevent over-thinking. Use 1,2 for the backswing and 1 for impact. The biggest problem when chipping is slowing down the clubhead just before impact, causing the hands to flip the club instead of keeping them ahead of the club at contact. Using the 1,2,1 will keep your hands moving as you come back to the ball.

The reason chipping can be a mental challenge is because it involves a slower swing and the distance relies on the amount of backswing, as well as "feel". Feel is dependent on practice and repetition. You have to train the brain with repetitive movements to acquire feel. The basal ganglia near the center of the brain controls rhythm for movement. The more you repeat the same motion, the better chance to repeat this same movement.

Visualization and repetition are the solutions for good chipping. I previously discussed visualization earlier suggesting closing your eyes while chipping to learn the process. When practicing anything on the range you should mimic the entire procedure you will use on the course. In other words, use the same routine before making a shot when practicing. IF YOU PRACTICE THE WAY YOU

PLAY, YOU WILL PLAY THE WAY YOU PRACTICED! This profound statement applies to every facet of the game.

How to practice and how to train the mind are the keys to success. Every day is a different day when you tee it up on the golf course. How you play each time is dependent on so many factors. Did you get enough sleep? Are you worried about something in your personal life? Are you experiencing some pain in your back? Is your job creating major stress right now? The list may be long. What can you do to forget all these distractions when you arrive at the course?

The best way to eliminate distractions is to add a sense of rhythm for the mental approach to golf and all that you do. Have you ever noticed how much easier it is to accomplish a difficult task when your mind and body feel a certain rhythm? This is why we listen to music while working on a creative or demanding project. Why do we perform better while using rhythm? When the brain places the chemical dopamine into our bloodstream we can generally function at our highest level. With a cadence in our movement we feel more confidence. A sense of calmness allows our brain to accomplish so much more. Without distractions and a sense of calm, the involuntary movements produced by the motor cortex and cerebellum can function with the accuracy needed to make the ideal golf swing. It's time to avoid distractions and feel the rhythm to make our game less stressful. It's time to enjoy the moment. When practicing, it would be to your advantage to listen to music, hum a favorite song, or just sense a beat in your mind. If you do this often, you will discover that your mind will function much better than ever before. Move with a beat or rhythm as you perform your setup routine. You will soon realize your game is improving without the physical effort you totally relied on in the past. And, when you put in the extra effort, the rhythm in your mind will make the process a simple task.

A routine should start when you arrive at the course, not when standing behind the ball to begin the setup process. When you arrive at the course you step out of your car, and you already have rhythm as you walk to the clubhouse. If you can carry this rhythm with you until the time you tee off, you will feel relaxed and confident. If you warm up before your round, start with easy swinging clubs such as wedges, or practice chipping. Start with clubs that require more feel to reach the target. This will encourage better timing with your longer clubs, driver, and fairway metals. It is important to have a certain feel when warming up, whether you are putting or hitting your driver. The rhythmic feel will carry over to your entire game for that day.

When putting, it is sometimes good to practice with a cadence of one, two in the back of your mind. One, swing back, two, contact the ball. By thinking one, two, you are adding music to your swing. By adding this counting beat you are establishing a feel for the greens and you are cementing that feel into your mind with the thought of the prescribed rhythm needed for the course on that particular day. This is especially good for longer putts. Personally, I use counting while playing on the course, if I have a sense of uncertainty with a difficult shot.

After the warm-up session, it's time to tee-off on the first hole. Having established a rhythm for the day you are in the proper state of mind. Just stay with your normal routine and your entire round should be a breeze.

It is important to practice your routine just like you practice every other facet of your game. Your setup routine can be rehearsed at home or at the range. Once a chosen club is removed from your golf bag, it is imperative you no longer think about swing thoughts. The most significant part of the routine is to avoid any thoughts that can interrupt the rhythm of the process. This would include not thinking about failed shots from an earlier hole. Any distractions from a normal routine will change everything about the flow of your thinking. If you are relaxed, the brain will function more effectively.

It's best to take a few deep breaths and feel relaxed as you start your routine. It is optional, but you may want to make a few practice swings before starting your routine. The practice swing(s) should be 50%-60% of your normal swing speed. Your objectives are to feel the weight of the clubhead, and to establish a rhythm. It is good to feel the weight of the clubhead during a practice swing because it will improve your timing when swinging at your normal speed. You can also add deep breathing while making a couple practice swings. You should practice breathing with your entire setup routine because the proper use of breathing will produce relaxation as you prepare to swing. Work on breathing techniques at the range, or at home without a ball.

The following is the explanation of a typical routine. Of course, you should develop your own personal routine since it must feel right for "your" game. Start by placing the ball on the tee. Next, stand behind the ball and take a deep breath, while picturing in your mind the contact of the ball and seeing it fly to your planned target. Then look down at the ball and imagine the line the ball needs to travel. Find a spot two to three feet in front of the ball as your aim line. Some golfers will establish their grip while behind the ball, and that can reduce the time at the address position. Next, move to the side of the ball and establish your clubface angle, and then position your body to align with the near target spot and the clubface. Rock your body slightly to establish a connection to the ground. You need to get the weight of your body in position for the swing. During this time, you should waggle the club to help sense the feel of the clubhead and to feel a tempo. Now it's time to make the final preparation to start the swing. Look one final time at the target, but this time, take a snapshot in your mind of the target. Or you can picture the flight of the ball, and the spot where it will land. This is your last chance to secure in your mind the most important thought in your routine, the TARGET. If you want to look at the target several times that is okay as long as you are memorizing the target. Next, take a deep breath and return your eyes to the ball, visualize the target in your mind, and start the swing.

It's important to develop your own routine, and then practice the routine enough to develop a sense of rhythm. It is also important to keep the routine as short as possible. The shorter routine will often prevent the emergence of negative thoughts and distractions. Do not change your routine for every shot, thus it is no longer a routine. Any minor change may affect the flow of your thinking, allowing time for unwanted thoughts to interrupt the process.

Chapter 6
Taking it to the Course

"Of all the hazards, fear is the worst."

Sam Snead

You have read golf books, taken lessons, practiced at the range, viewed golf videos, and studied psychology. Now it's time to "take it to the course". But, for some reason, you tee-off on the first hole at your home course and your ball goes into the lake, like it did so many times before. It is always difficult to understand why some things never change. I have had this happen many times. There is this one hole, and for some reason you always have some type of problem. Sometimes you have to accept that the hole is jinxed. You think to yourself, I am going to the range this week, and I am going to pretend that I am playing this particular hole. I will practice until I feel like I have finally slayed the dragon. Guess what? Next time out, the ball goes into the lake again. When this happens you think about Albert Einstein's favorite line, "The definition of insanity is, doing the same thing over and over and expecting different results." I have to believe Einstein was playing golf when he formulated this statement. According to an article published by the Augusta Chronicle, Einstein was asked by journalist, John Derr, "Do you play golf?" Einstein's response was, "No, no, I tried it once. Too complicated. I quit". Eventually after going down the path of failure too many times, you accept mediocrity. It's time to turn your game around!

For some reason most golfers hit great shots on the range, but when you go out to the course, they feel like Dr. Jekyll turned into Mr. Hyde. Finally, you realize, "Golf, it's all mental". I have experienced this same dilemma. After extensive reading in the field of psychology, along with first-hand experience, and of course, common sense, it is not difficult to understand what mental challenges golfers are dealing with on the course. Every golfer I have ever spoken to will tell me, "I don't understand it, I can hit almost every shot great at the range, but when I go to the course my game falls apart." Why does this happen? The frequent answer is that you were more relaxed and you were not really aiming at a specific target. Plus, you were using the same club for several shots in a row, and therefore it required less effort to be consistent. These answers are all correct, but the main reason for this failure is that your thought process is all wrong. When we attempt to take the shots on the range to the course we expect the same results.

There is no greater pressure than what we implant into ourselves. Pressure that is self- inflicted far exceeds any stress you experience on the course. Ninety percent of the tension you feel on the course is created by yourself being you own critic. This mental part of golf is common to every golfer, including professionals. You are often your own worst enemy on the golf course. Depending on your level of expectations, it will determine the extent of this dilemma. People who strive for perfection will suffer the consequences more than anyone. This can be the biggest problem for professional golfers when their game is below their normal standard. The player is manufacturing their own demise. It is all a state of mind, and it only takes a few bad rounds to change your self-perception. What started as a small problem will often become a "slump".

If the golfer can just slightly lower their expectations, then the desire for perfection can be avoided. Another way to look at the issue is to rethink the situation from a new perspective. If you can lower expectations a small amount you will have a better opportunity to attain near perfection by letting the mind focus on the "now" and not results. The golfer that is result oriented will always be playing with excessive self-inflicted pressure.

So how does a person overcome this habit of excessive self-appraisal? You would think that most of the tension in golf would come from other players in your foursome. But for most golfers, most all the tension is self-induced and has nothing to do with the other golfers. This can be true for other sports, but not to the same degree. Other than tennis, most of the other sports are team sports. With team sports each player contributes to the effort to win. Players can excel in team sports without as much pressure. The pressure is shared with other players. In team sports there is also less time to think about a given situation. When pro golfers participate in the Ryder Cup matches they are more expressive in their desire to win. They are rooting for players on their team that are normally adversaries. Most of the players on the Ryder Cup teams seem to play better than playing their regular golf tournaments. This occurs because of the reduced opportunity to focus on their own self-criticism. Consider for a moment, how often have you seen a golfer throw a club in disgust when playing in a scramble or any team event? This leads into this profound statement. The greatest cause for failure at golf is being your own critic while playing.

Back to the question, how do I prevent this self-defeating criticism? Here are some ways to help eliminate the problem. First, do not set hard to attain goals before and while playing. Secondly, play in the "now". Do not think about results because you can't control what hasn't happened yet. Thirdly, do not try to compare practice to being on the course. Practice does not affect score, so why think about it. Fourthly, do not critique individual shots. Wait until after the round is over before evaluating. Lastly, stop for a moment and think, golf is a game. It is not a life or death situation. It was invented for the purpose of having fun for a few hours and then returning to your home and recalling all the great moments you had with friends. If you can make the necessary adjustments in thinking by following these recommendations, over time you will be a much better golfer, and you will have greater enjoyment in the process.

So you are waiting to tee-off on the first hole. You've been joking with friends in your foursome and now it's your turn to put your ball on the tee and swing away. Your warm-up was horrible and the others that tee-off are already in the fairway. "No pressure", you think to yourself. You place the ball on the tee and you start your normal routine. You're thinking, "I've got this, no problem". You are settled in your setup and about to start the swing, when out of the blue, you recall last week's shot into the woods on the left. You focus intently on the ball and target, and you believe the "in the woods" thought is forgotten, so you swing away. As you predicted, you watch the ball hook into the woods exactly as it did the previous time. You try to joke about it with your friends, "There must be a magnet pulling my ball into the woods every time I play this hole!" They laugh, but now you started the round feeling like "crap". You have lost confidence and it's just the first hole!

This happens so often in golf that it is almost the norm. The problem at this point, you have become embarrassed and upset, making the next few shots a greater challenge. One bad shot at the beginning of the round can sometimes ruin the rest of your day.

How do you change this situation you created? This has nothing to do with the other players. In golf, only you are in full control of what transpires. There are days that, no matter what, bad things just happen. You might have had little sleep the night before, you may have stress at work, or you may have muscle pains. Some things are out of your control, so you have to accept the consequences. On those days, just try to enjoy your day as much as possible and not be serious about how you perform. We are all human, and it is okay to have those days that you cannot control the mental part of your game.

As I discussed in the previous chapter, there is a procedure for keeping your game in check. If you arrive at the course in the right frame of mind, anything is possible. Having a good setup routine is the best way to overcome adversity. You should practice a routine regularly at the range so it is natural on the course.

By now, you have come to realize how the power of the brain can enhance your game. And at the same time, it can destroy it. Being in a relaxed state of mind will provide the opportunity to perform to the best of your ability.

As was discussed in previous chapters, your mind and body must be relaxed to perform well on the course. Your game during practice always feels so relaxed and you perform much better. There is another factor to consider for not performing as well on the course as you do on the range. How you practice may be affecting the outcome on the course. If you would spend 75% of your time on the range working specifically on tempo and timing, all the work you rehearsed on the range would finally show up on the course.

The key to better golf is to establish more "feel" with every shot. This can only happen if the mind and body are in sync. Fluidity is a training process. This does not mean you have to swing slower to accomplish this. Fluidity can exist with a fast swing as well. But the process for warm-up must start slower and gradually work up to your normal speed. This is what the pros do, and most amateurs do not. If you don't work on tempo and timing EVERY TIME at the range when making corrections for a swing issue, your swing will suffer greatly on the course. When making corrections on the range you must go back and forth between the swing change, and then timing. If tempo and timing are not the main part of your practice sessions you will not be able to "take it to the course".

The ultimate purpose of practice on the range should be to improve "feel". Without adding feel to your shot making, you will have accomplished little to improve your game. A statement to remember, "You cannot transfer swing mechanics from the range to the course unless it includes the mental thought of FEEL".

Feel in golf is not easy to define. Feel consists of many things: a sense of touch, visual acuity, mental certainty, and mental rhythm. A sense of touch is the nerves in your hands sensing contact with the club handle and also sensing the weight of the entire club, especially the clubhead. Visual acuity is seeing the ball, the grass below it, the club in your hands, the ultimate target, and subconsciously seeing some of the movement of the club as you swing. Mental certainty is a state of mind, which is the confidence attained by previously practicing specific repetitions of a particular movement. Mental rhythm is the result of training the brain to repeat effortless motions every time you move the body and club. If all these thoughts and actions take place during the swing, you will have accomplished a shot with a sense of "feel".

Since feel is so important for better golf, how can you improve the feel for a shot? Let's break down each one of the four characteristics of feel, starting with touch. To create a better sense of touch, all you have to do is think about it. If the brain is focused on touch, the nerves will become more sensitive. Start by gripping the club softly and direct your mind to sense the texture on the club handle. Light grip pressure and thinking about your hands softly holding the club will greatly improve your sense of touch. To feel the weight of the club, swing the club slightly forward before moving it back for the backswing. This forward movement creates a lag of the clubhead when changing direction. The lag is the force of inertia produced by the weight of the club. This is good for practice swings to help sense the weight of the clubhead. If you do this often you will begin to feel the sensation of the clubhead and this can transfer to the actual swing by memorizing the feel in your mind. You can do practice swings on the course using the same technique. You can also use several waggles during your setup routine. Feel the weight of the clubhead while you waggle the club. The greater the amount of feel you can create, the greater the opportunity to swing with more rhythm and fluidity. Your goal is to improve tempo and timing.

Next is improving visual acuity. To do this you must learn to become more aware of your surroundings. Your mind must become more aware of the how your surroundings affect the movement of your body. First, focus your eyes on the ball and the grass surrounding it. This will give you the perspective for how far away and how to align your body. See a picture in your mind of both the ball and the surrounding area. The more detail you include in the setup, the more vivid your mental recall. More memories will produce more recall. When you look at the target, imagine that it is a bullseye on a target board, as used for archery. The bullseye is laying on the green or fairway. The purpose for this can be explained with an analogy. If you were throwing dart, your mind sees the entire dartboard, then your eyes stare at the bullseye just before you throw the dart. When you perform the movements for this action you are totally unaware of your body's movements. Your mind is solely focused on the bullseye and your body moved automatically. If you can create more detail with mental images, you will be able to recall more information from past memories to repeat the same actions.

Mental certainty can be improved by simply doing more repetitions of the swing. This only works if the repetitions are correct and accurate. The golf swing can be complex, and the mind can become confused if you are thinking about the swing rather than the target as mentioned previously. Assuming you have the correct swing, then more practice will produce a confident repeatable swing. A confident mind is conducive to a repeatable swing, which results in more feel.

Mental rhythm is the result of having a mental sense for the movement of the club. If you can sense the presence of the club as it moves through space it will form a connection between you and club. There must be a connection if the body and club are to work as a unit. This is the result of mind being more aware of the club you are using to perform the swing. By increasing awareness you are able to feel more rhythm in the swing.

There are times in your golfing life you just need to take a break. This can sometimes be a better solution for improvement than practicing. If your game needs a fresh perspective for how to resolve issues with your swing or mental focus, it is always good to do a "reboot". If your mind can separate from the normal golf routine, you may have a clearer viewpoint after a few weeks away from the game. Many golfers who have constantly worked hard at their game will often feel like every ounce of energy has been drained from their body when out on the course. This is when you must realize, a break from golf is necessary. The cause for this loss of energy is entirely mental.

The brain is no different than the muscles in your body. There are times when rest and relaxation are the best medicine. Even though it may not be apparent, your mind is producing an excessive amount of the stress hormone, cortisol. By continuously striving to improve your game, your brain is causing your adrenal glands to secrete larger amounts of this hormone into the bloodstream. After a while, your body gets so used to this routine stress level that you begin to accept this state as your norm. By taking a break, you are cleansing both your mind and body. After a couple weeks away from golf, you will acquire a new outlook for all the challenges you were facing.

Cortisol creates many side effects that can greatly affect your golf game. Small amounts can actually be good for golf, but too much is a problem. Some of the side effects of higher levels of cortisol include: increased blood sugar levels, increased blood pressure, increased heart rate, muscle weakness, and depression. So the goal is to manage the amount of cortisol and maintain this hormone at lower levels. This can be done by: getting more sleep, more exercise, reduce caffeine intake, improve diet, indulge in hobbies, become involved in music or art, and practice deep breathing exercises. This sounds just like R & R as the cure. So, if you want to improve your golf game, maybe you just need to "reboot"!

Chapter 7

Training Drills
for
Mind and Body

"Hit the shot you think you can hit. Not the one
you think you should."

Dr. Bob Rotella

Now that you have a good understanding of how the brain can control your game, it's time to use this knowledge to your advantage. The brain can be trained to produce a great golf swing. Training will involve breaking down the swing into 6 parts. By segmenting the swing, it is possible to establish the correct movements for each part and then put all these pieces together. The idea for this training is to use slow motion drills for each part, and then repeat these drills many times so that these motions become etched into the brain. When each part feels natural and can be performed with little thought, then you can combine the parts for the complete swing. The six parts will include Setup, Takeaway, Full Turn, Transition, Impact, and Follow-through.

IDEAL SETUP   IDEAL BACKSWING

SETUP

The setup plus all the following photos are shown using a 7-iron. The setup starts with the feet near shoulder width apart. It is preferred that the left foot be angled about 30% toward the target. This helps the body turn through and around after impact. The ball position should be about 3 inches inside the left heel. The ball is more centered for wedges and just Inside the left heel for the driver and fairway woods. The upper body has a slight tilt to the right. The head position should be slightly behind the ball line. The elbows should be fairly close together. The left elbow points toward the left hip and the right elbow points toward the right hip. The left arm is straight and is close to the line of the club shaft. The arms hang almost straight down form the shoulders when gripping the club. For longer shafted clubs this distance will increase slightly. As much as 4-5 inches for the driver and fairway woods. The head is level and should remain close to the same position from setup and until just past impact. Your weight should be over the your arches and distributed approximately 50/50 over both feet. The feet, knees, hips, and shoulders should align with the target. When bending at the waist, the back should be fairly straight as you address the ball and throughout the swing. The right knee must be bend slightly and pointed inward.

TAKEAWAY DRILL

This is a critical part of the swing. The takeaway will determine swing tempo, swing plane, width of arc, wrist angles and promotes a straight left arm. This slow motion drill starts with a good setup position and ends when the hands are just below hip high. Move the arms, hands, arms, and club back together as a unit. While moving the club, maintain the same wrist position from setup until your hands are outside the right hip. The hands should pass over the toe of the right shoe. The toe of the club should point forward about 30% as it nears hip high. The one-piece takeaway is done by rotating your shoulders similar to a putting stroke. Be sure the club head starts moving low to the ground to encourage a wider arc. This rotation of the shoulders should feel like the upper body is rotating around your core. The core of your body is located near the lower waist area. Perform this drill 15 times. Take a break and repeat the process again. Be sure to study the photo.

FULL TURN DRILL

This part of the swing drills begins at waist high and ends at the top of the backswing. As the hands and club approach waist high during the backswing, the wrists start to cock. The wrists cock gradually as your hands near chest high. The wrists should be cocked near 90% once your hands are shoulder high. The right arm must push out during this part of the swing to maintain a straight left arm. Your weight shifts to the inside of the right foot when the club is waist high and eventually moves onto the right heel as the club nears the top of the swing. The photo shows the right knee remaining bent similar to the setup position. This is the anchor for the backswing. This will cause the hips and upper body to coil like a spring. Be sure to complete the backswing. The back of the left wrist must be flat at the top of the swing and the right elbow more downward. Perform this drill 15 times and repeat.

TRANSITION DRILL

This drill starts at the top of the backswing and ends when the club shaft is near level and points toward the target. The biggest difference between amateurs and pros is the transition move. This move starts by shifting weight to the left side onto the left foot. When the weight shifts forward, the upper body starts to unwind. The club head hesitates as the shoulders begin turning. Try to sense the weight of the clubhead when the shoulders start to turn. Next, the hands and the right elbow drop down to the right side of the body. The right wrist must maintain the cocked position from the top of the swing. When the hands are waist high, they start pulling the club handle down toward the ball. The club shaft is now level and pointing toward the target. The right hand will appear to be in a hand shake position, still cocked and ready to release the clubhead through impact. Perform the drill 15 times and then repeat the process.

IMPACT DRILL

This part of the swing drill begins with the club shaft pointing straight at the target (level position - photo shows slightly below level). The right wrist that was cocked now pushes down toward the ball. Note the position of the hands in front of the left hip just before impact. Timing is important to attain the forward shaft lean of approximately 10% at impact. Do half swing drills matching the positions shown. After impact be sure to extend the right arm fully toward the target. Imagine shaking hands with someone standing next to your left side. For the drill, swing from waist high to waist high in the follow-through. Be sure to maintain head position, down and slightly behind the ball line. The right shoulder will bring the head up as it passes below your chin. Maintaining this head position is very significant for this part of the swing to be successful. Perform this drill 15 times and repeat.

FOLLOW-THROUGH DRILL

This part of the swing starts from impact to the end of the swing. Start from the impact position and focus on maintaining head position with full extension, again using the concept of shaking hands with someone on your left side in front of you. The force of the swing will pull the hands and club around your body. At the end of the swing the belt buckle should face the target. The left leg is straight and the right knee should touch or almost touch the inside of the left knee. The arms move around the upper body and the left elbow points to the ground and the club shaft comes to a stop at the back of the neck. Perform this drill 15 times and repeat.

FULL SWING
(Front View)

Setup Takeaway Full Turn

Transition Impact Extension

Follow-through

The takeaway shows the hands, arms, shoulders, and club moving together while maintaining the grip angles. The wrists do not begin to cock until hands are outside the right hip. At the top of the swing, a full turn of the of the shoulders moves the weight to the right side. You can see the twisting of the back and hips promotes the release of energy back to the left side for impact.

FULL SWING
(Rear View)

Setup   **Takeaway**   **Full Turn**

Transition   **Impact**

Follow-through

The setup shows knee bend with perfect posture and alignment. During takeaway, the clubface angle is slightly closed. The left wrist is flat at the top of the swing. The full turn positions the club shaft near level. During transition, the hands and club have dropped down and the right wrist remains cocked. The impact position shows the upper body maintaining spine angle through contact with the ball. Follow-through shows full extension.

FINAL THOUGHTS

Fifty years ago, golf had many great professional players, but today's competition has elevated to a point that there is normally a different winner every week. What separates the performance of these great players is difficult to ascertain. The winner is often the player that happens to be "on their game" for that particular week. Even then, the winner is not determined until the last few holes on the final day of the tournament.

Still, there are a handful of players that are near the top of the leaderboard almost every time they play. What is so special about this small group of players? This is what I have chosen to evaluate at the conclusion of this book. These players have certain inherent physical and mental skills that must be better than other excellent professionals. Based on what has been presented in this book, what mental skills are shared among these great players?

Each of these players possess a specific skill, even though they all share the ability to win. Just to name a few: Rory McIlroy is outstanding off the tee. Jordan Spieth has an amazing short game. Nelly Korda is an accurate wedge player. Scottie Scheffler is a great iron player. Cameron Smith can putt with amazing accuracy. In addition, there were many historic players, such as: Bobby Jones had a graceful transition, producing the most relaxed swing. Ben Hogan developed the pure refinement of the golf swing. Sam Snead had a smooth oily swing with power and accuracy. Arnold Palmer had a strong quick swing that rivaled the best in the game. Jack Nicklaus excelled in visualization and focus and he knew how to win. Tiger

Woods had tremendous power and accuracy that dominated golf for two decades (Tiger is still playing). Having these greater skills is (was) still not the primary reason why they held a trophy more often than other great players.

Each of the greatest players possess(ed) a different type of mental approach that is (was) an edge above the others. One thing in common is (was) their ability to bounce back when confronted with adversity. Another, is (was) their ability to win. They find a way to win, even when they are (were) not playing their best. And lastly, they can better analyze and focus on the shots required to achieve success. If you look closely at these superior traits, they are "all mental". The ultimate superiority in golf is determined by how well a player controls the mental aspect of the game.

The first reason for greatness is the ability to "bounce back". The ability to forget the missed 3-foot putt on the previous hole requires a very special mental skill. Nearly all golfers would not be able to forget this type of blunder when the game is on the line. Whenever Jordan Spieth misses a short putt, he normally scores a birdie on the next hole. The superior golfer is always forward-thinking. Earlier, I went into great detail about being your own worst enemy on the course by critiquing your game. You cannot criticize yourself on the course for a mistake or miscalculation. Once something happens, you must move on. You cannot change the past. These special players do not think about the past while playing. They think only about getting a birdie on the next hole. I can often recall seeing Rory McIlroy smile on his way to the next hole after missing a crucial putt. He was already thinking about hitting a great drive and wedge shot, and getting a birdie or eagle on the next hole. If you can visualize in your mind what you need to do in the future to make up for a sudden mistake, you will become more "driven" to excel and compensate for what just happened. For these players, they choose to excel when others give up. This is not complicated. It is just a better way to approach how the game should be played. These players have great confidence. They use adversity to gain strength. The next time you miss a 3-foot putt, don't get upset. Instead, do what the pros do; think about getting a birdie on the next hole. Always use "forward thinking". Forget about negative results, and instead think about positive future possibilities.

Next, these special players think they have to win. Second place is not an option. This desire to win cannot be taught by the best golf instructors. These few golfers are born with this attitude. It is part of their DNA. There may have been a few who acquired this personality trait, but if they did, this likely occurred in early childhood. A better way to describe this trait is that these players do not want to lose. The desire to win is about giving "your all" to accomplish a goal and prove to yourself that you are better than anyone else at whatever activity you are competing in at that given moment. These players have the ability to persevere. When faced with 20-footers for par they often sink these putts, even though the tour average is just 15%. The best players in the world have the mental stamina to find a way to WIN when the odds are not in their favor.

If you want to improve your own game and your desire to win, the best method is to improve confidence. This will require hard work and determination. There are no shortcuts for improvement. The mental portion of your golf game is dependent on how well you perform the golf swing. Taking lessons and extensive practice will increase confidence, and your mental game will become an advantage instead of a liability. If you have confidence, it will enhance your desire to win.

The last reason for this greatness is the ability to analyze and focus on the "now" while anticipating a positive outcome for superior confidence. The greatest players, when preparing to hit a shot on the course have a look in their eyes that is unlike the average professional player. What are they thinking that puts them "into the zone" on almost every attempted shot? Just like the best in the world in other sports, they approach every shot as if were the final shot of the game when it's all on the line. Nothing else matters to them at that moment in time, except producing excellence by using every skill they learned and practiced since childhood. I spoke about focus and visualization throughout this book because these mental skills are what produced the greatest players ever to play the game. It is difficult to understand this special trait because excellent focus is dependent on so many factors. The best golfers have that special look in their eyes because they are visualizing the golf ball flying off the clubface and then foresee the ball land at the target they have perceived. In their mind, the image is so vivid that it has already happened. This may be the most important reason why these golfers are among the greatest of all time.

One thing that is special about golf, all these players publicly display grace when losing an important match. But once they leave the course, they cannot help but think about the one or two mistakes that contributed to their defeat. Ultimately, they accept the loss as a learning experience for becoming an even better player. Bobby Jones once said, "I never learned anything from a match I won". The greatest players must be our model for physical and mental training to achieve excellence. If we can incorporate some of the knowledge of these extraordinary players, we will profoundly enhance our enjoyment of this great game.

Acknowledgements

Reference Books that provided some of the quotes and thoughts in the text of this book include:

"Golf My Way" by Jack Nicklaus.

"Ben Hogan's Secret Fundamental" by Larry Miller.

"Welcome to the Brain" by Sandra Aamodt and Sam Wang.

"Simply the Brain"- DK Publishing

Quotations at the beginning of each chapter were obtained on-line from three sources: Kidadl.com, Southern California Golf Association (scga.com), and GolfWRX.com

All Photos: iStockPhoto.com
Front Cover – Who_I_am
Back Cover – VasjaKoman
Fig. 1- ttsz, **Fig. 2** – Sunshine_Art, **Fig. 3** – wetcake,
Fig. 4 –whitehoune, **Fig. 5** – ttsz, **Fig. 6** – Marisvector,
Fig. 7 – Kittisak-Taramas, **Fig. 8** – Ball in Head – fatido,
Scene in Head – Pavel Konnikov, **Fig. 9** – Edwin Tan
Fig. 10 – Pool – brianbigel, Archery – snoofek, Darts – Ivenok,
Range – Andrew Krauchenko, **Fig. 11** – Ball in Flight –
Taveesakrsi, Ball on Tee – robynmac
Chapter photos of hole and ball – CGinspiration
Chapter 7 photos: Setup/Backswing – nattrass
Chapter 7 sequence photos: provided by 4x6
Final Thoughts: Rossella Apostoli